RELIGION AND SPORTS IN AMERICAN CULTURE

Religion and Sports in American Culture explores the relationship between religion and modern sports in America. Whether found in the religious purpose of ancient Olympic Games, in curses believed to plague the Chicago Cubs, or in the figure of Tim Tebow, religion and sports have been and are still tightly intertwined. While there is widespread suspicion that sports is slowly encroaching on the territory historically occupied by religion, Scholes and Sassower assert that sports is not replacing religion and that nor is sports a religion. Instead, the authors look at the relationship between sports and religion in America from a post-secular perspective that looks at both discourses as a part of the same cultural web. In this way each institution is able to maintain its own integrity, legitimacy, and unique expression of cultural values as they relate to each other. Utilizing important themes that intersect both religion and sports, Scholes and Sassower illuminate the complex and often publicly contentious relationship between the two.

Appropriate for both classroom use and for the interested non-specialist, *Religion and Sports in American Culture* brings pilgrimage, sacrifice, relics, and redemption together in an unexpected cultural continuity.

Jeffrey Scholes is Assistant Professor in the Philosophy Department at the University of Colorado, Colorado Springs. He is the Director of the Center for Religious Diversity and Public Life at UCCS. His areas of interest include American religion and political economy as well as religion and popular culture. He is the author of *Vocation and the Politics of Work: Work and Popular Theology in a Consumer Culture* (2013).

Raphael Sassower is Professor of Philosophy at the University of Colorado, Colorado Springs. His areas of interest include postmodern technoscience, digital culture, and the philosophy of the social sciences (primarily economics). Among his latest publications are *Postcapitalism: Moving Beyond Ideology in America's Economic Crisis* (2009) and *War Images: Fabricating Reality* (2010).

RELIGION AND SPORTS IN AMERICAN CULTURE

Jeffrey Scholes and Raphael Sassower

Routledge
Taylor & Francis Group

NEW YORK AND LONDON

First published 2014
by Routledge
711 Third Avenue, New York, NY 10017

and by Routledge
2 Park Square, Milton Park, Abingdon, Oxon OX14 4RN

Routledge is an imprint of the Taylor & Francis Group, an informa business

Library of Congress Cataloging in Publication Data
   Scholes, Jeffrey, 1971–
   Religion and sports in American culture/by Jeffrey Scholes and
   Raphael Sassower.—First edition.
   pages cm
   Includes bibliographical references and index.
   1. Sports—Religious aspects. 2. Sports in popular culture—
   United States. 3. Athletes—Religious life. I. Sassower, Raphael.
   II. Title.
   GV706.42.S55 2013
   796.01—dc23
   2012050300

ISBN: 978-0-415-64531-7 (hbk)
ISBN: 978-0-415-64532-4 (pbk)
ISBN: 978-0-203-07566-1 (ebk)

Typeset in Bembo
by Florence Production Limited, Stoodleigh, Devon, UK

CONTENTS

ACKNOWLEDGMENTS

We'd like to thank those whose expertise in the area helped guide our endeavor, including Professors Jay Coakley, Paul Harvey, and Jeff de Montez Oca. Likewise, we are grateful to Rose Lyda who read and gave valuable feedback on parts of our manuscript in its early stages. Professor Dan Clanton read the entire manuscript and meticulously assisted us in eliminating some errors and adding relevant missing information. Gina Perenchio helped tremendously in the final editing of the book. Our editor at Routledge, Dr. Steve Wiggins, has shepherded this intellectual journey from inception to completion. We are grateful for his trust and patience.

Lastly, we'd like to thank the University of Colorado, Colorado Springs in general, and our philosophy department in particular, for encouraging the kind of collegial collaboration that would be the envy of *any* sports team.

INTRODUCTION

Sports stories capture a nation's attention most often when they involve important events such as the Super Bowl, World Series, or Olympic Games. Or sometimes these stories become a part of American lore when they chronicle amazing athletic feats such as Roger Bannister cracking the four-minute mile barrier or Joe DiMaggio getting a hit in 56 straight baseball games. In addition, much attention is paid to acts of indiscretion such as Tiger Woods' marital infidelity throughout his remarkable golf career or Lance Armstrong's use of performance-enhancing drugs during his seven Tour de France victories. Rarely is the nation enrapt with a team winning games in the middle of a season or an athlete who has neither broken a hallowed record nor fallen from grace. Yet, in the middle of the 2011 National Football League season, Tim Tebow, a less-than-stellar quarterback as far as mechanics and statistics go, did just that. What made the Tebow story newsworthy was the possible relationship between his strong faith and the logic-defying wins that he helped engineer for the Denver Broncos that year. This had news commentators for major media outlets and many in the public at large asking an unusual question: Is it possible that Tebow's faith can explain a series of unlikely victories on the football field? Or more generally, is there a real, tangible link between sports and religion?

Many athletes have cited their faith as a crucial component of their athletic performance to a national audience before; the 2011 Broncos are not the only team to have defied incredible odds to make the playoffs, and Tebow's chances of playing for another NFL team look slim (at the time of this writing). Yet in the fall of 2011 and early in 2012, the spectre of religion and sports actually intersecting provoked the ire of skeptics and the cheers of his supporters with a level of passion unseen in recent memory.

Yes, certain statements and actions of coaches, owners, and athletes have always sparked heated debate among sports fans and the media, but Tebow throws religious fuel on this fire; the supernatural on top of the natural. Wildly varying, yet strongly held opinions on Tebow seem to stem from the odd coupling of a presumably secular activity, sports, with the presumably sacred stuff of religion. The "oil and water" view seeks to keep matters of faith private and off the football field, where public displays of athleticism and determination are the real factors in wins and losses. This view expresses itself as uncomfortability with translating successes on the field into statements about God. A headline from *U.S. News and World Report* during Tebow's 2011 season sums it up: "God Has Better Things to Do than Worry about Tim Tebow."

Certainly, sports history is littered with legendary athletes that have risen to iconic, almost saintly, status. Fans follow them, hang onto every word they utter, pay exorbitant sums for tickets and memorabilia, and take pilgrimages to Halls of Fame to catch a glimpse of their old uniforms and equipment. Yet despite religious-like devotion to sports, most fans would stop short of calling sports a religion or an athlete a saint. God does not pull for Tim Tebow, Michael Jordan is a far cry from Mother Teresa, and devotion to a favorite player or team will not save souls, according to this view. As Robert Higgs and Michael Braswell put it, "however remarkably well certain athletes may unify mind, body, and soul, and there are many we know who do, there is still no argument for elevating to divine status the games in which they participate" (Higgs and Braswell 2004, 4).

Alternatively, there are some who hold more of a "peanut butter and jelly" view that trumpets the mixing of religion and sports (Higgs and Braswell 2004, 1, 15). For instance, Tebow's success on the field is proof positive that God blesses those who are pious and obedient. His failures merely indicate that God is testing him (and his fans). And even the die-hard Broncos fan who prefers to leave religion to the Church was probably open to the possibility that "something else" was at work in Tebow's comebacks. As long as her team wins, the actual means to achieve victory is less relevant than the end. To lend credence to this view, religion and sports, in fact, have had a long-standing, intimate relationship. The ancient Mayans' sacrifice of the losers of a ball game to their gods and the earliest Olympics serving as athletic offerings to the Greek gods reveal that the need to separate religion from sports is one that developed rather than being given to us.

By the time of the early Christian Church, the way that sports was used to convey spiritual truths illustrates a new way that religion and sports were intersecting. Paul, in his first letter to the Corinthians, states:

> Do you not know that in a race all the runners run, but only one gets the prize? Run in such a way as to get the prize. Everyone who competes in the games goes into strict training. They do it to get a crown that will not last: but we do it to get a crown that will last forever.
>
> (1 Corinthians 9:24–25)

Much later, Billy Sunday, an evangelist at the turn of the twentieth century and ex-professional baseball player, would address his congregation in his old uniform to deliver a sermon. And Billy Graham has told audiences, perhaps provocatively so, that, "Jesus was the greatest athlete who has ever lived" (Twitchell and Ross 2008, 230). When sports is used in all of these ways, it operates as a metaphor; it conveys a religious idea, but is not the main focus of the statement for those using it. Hence, when we read between the lines of this kind of use of sports language it is clear that religious truth is more important than the example from sports that merely helps demonstrate the "real" point.

Yet sports would not be utilized for religious purposes if it did not resonate strongly with the public then and today. What are we to make of the fact that twenty-one of the top forty-six most watched television broadcasts of all time are Super Bowls and that a sporting event may be the best vehicle for international diplomacy—the Olympics? Instead, it may be that sports has overtaken religion in the battle for hearts and minds, no matter what a local pastor may claim. And while sports is unavoidable in American culture today, since nine in ten Americans still believe in God, religion doesn't seem to be going away either. Because both religion and sports occupy such a prominent space in American culture, putting one above the other is not as simple as one might think. Is it possible for sports and religion to share the same cultural space as powerful authorities, or can there be only one sheriff in town?

We argue in this book that the best way to think about the relationship between religion and sports in America is not as separate discourses that compete with each other for cultural ascendency. Instead, we contend that by analyzing those junctures where sports and religion overlap or where they share a similar vocabulary, even though the means of expression may differ greatly, a fuller understanding of the current-day relationship emerges. We base our contention on the mounting evidence that the sacred and the secular do not operate in two separate domains in twenty-first century culture and then apply this insight to religion and sports. If one is unable to locate and cleanly separate the religious from the non-religious, as was once thought possible, then the battle between religion and sports (or any secular activity) is largely exaggerated by those looking for a fight. What is the support for such a claim that, admittedly, may strike the reader as odd and out of step with reality?

The Sacred and the Secular Today

Regarding the sharing of a vocabulary, Catherine Albanese argues that certain "codes of living" that have been historically managed by religion can be now found in transmitters of "cultural religion" in America such as sports, technology, literature, and modern psychology. For Albanese, sports "mark out a separate area for their activities— 'playground or sacred space'" that invites participants into a "miniature rehearsal for the game of life" that is "a struggle between contesting forces in which there is a winning and a losing side" (Albanese 1992, 475). Sports does not simply constitute a time for play when the workday is done. Rather, it is the ability of sports to write these deeply entrenched codes that nourish the link between self-denial and success, build moral character, and teach how to lose with dignity. And these lessons are enforced by values such as "loyalty, fair play, and being a 'good sport' in losing" before, during, and after a game (Ibid., 476). In this way, sports fulfills one of the primary *functions* of religion (the instruction of ethical behavior), yet does so without taking over that jurisdiction from religion entirely. Religion and sports are not in competition with each other for who gets the right to teach such values; each can accomplish this function in its own way and even draw on each other, if needed, as Paul did 2,000 years ago. By emphasizing the common function of religion and sports, the question of that which gives rise to these values (God or respect for the game) becomes less important than the ways that these functions are expressed in culture. But why take culture so seriously in attempting to understand the relationship between religion and sports, and how does culture put them in relationship in the first place?

Anthropologist Clifford Geertz describes a human being as "an animal suspended in webs of significance he himself has spun, I take culture to be those webs" (Geertz 1977, 5). In other words, we create culture (art, music, literature, movies, technology, products, and language, to name a few cultural artifacts) but are also bound by that which we create. New fibers of a web can be spun that create different cultural pathways, but they are always corralled by the constraints of the cultural medium. Indeed, that cultural product can spin back and guide one down this or that pathway. A creative poem is still bound by the language in which it is written and the poem, instead of standing as a freely created product alone, can continue to affect future poets in their writing.

Applying Geertz's metaphor to religion and sports, Albanese asserts that both are part of a "web of interrelated cultural forms" (Ibid., 476). They are two sets of institutions and traditions, customs and values, ceremonies and rituals that inform each other in one culture or web. Not only are they both cultural forms, as she says, but they are also part of the same network. If we extend the metaphor again, we may think of sports and religion as two spiders on the same web. They are different spiders but when one moves on the web, the other is affected by the movement of the thread. And because, according to Geertz, the web is one of cultural significance and meanings, both sports and religion must, at times, utilize the same pathways and channels on the web to get where they are going. With the internet and digital media, we have a more elaborate web that allows for quicker movement and access to other parts of the web. But just because religion and sports now may move in the same cultural web, they still don't *have* to communicate with each other, or spiders can keep to themselves. Or it still may be the case that religion does other, very important things for people that sports simply cannot do, such as save souls, and therefore there may be barriers that prevent an open, somewhat equal relationship.

However, a brief look at the historical relationship between the religious and the secular in America suggests that the tactic of separating the secular from the religious (or spider from spider) with strict lines of demarcation and high barriers is simply no longer possible. Institutional religion faced little threat to its authority for most of human history in large part because there simply was not a separation, and hence potential for a contest, between the sacred and the secular. Beginning in seventeenth-century Europe, science, with its power to describe and predict nature, began to differentiate itself from the religious realm and replace the authority of the Church and the Bible to explain the universe. Of course religion still existed in the following centuries, but its growing inability to affect public life relegated it to the private realm of the individual. The theory of secularization put forth by scholars in the latter half of the twentieth century predicted that religion would continue to lose the battle with the secular world and eventually die out completely. Peter Berger describes the process like this:

> By secularization, we mean the process by which sectors of society and culture are removed from the domination of religious institutions and symbols . . . It [secularization] affects the totality of cultural life and of ideation, and may be observed in the decline of religious contents in the arts, in philosophy, in literature and, most important of all, in the rise of science as an autonomous, thoroughly secular perspective on the world . . . Put simply, this

means that the modern West has produced an increasing number of individuals who look upon the world and their own lives without the benefit of religious interpretations.

(Berger 1967, 107–108)

Religion's disappearing act from the public square meant that secular institutions such as the state or science could now do the work previously ascribed to religion, whether it be explaining the world, fostering social bonds, or even guiding ethical behavior. Religion and the secular are "silo-ed" here, with the secular silo growing and the religion one shrinking day by day.

This process and impact of secularization, however, was far from uniform across Western civilization. As has been noted frequently, the United States, while integrating many Enlightenment principles into its political structure, maintained a high level of religiosity into the twenty-first century, unlike much of Europe. As José Casanova states:

[T]he United States was born as a modern secular state, never knew the established church of the European caesaro-papist absolutist state, and did not need to go through a European process of secular differentiation in order to become a modern secular society . . . the United States has always been the paradigmatic form of a modern secular, differentiated society. Yet the triumph of "the secular" came aided by religion rather than at its expense, and the boundaries themselves became so diffused that, at least by European ecclesiastical standards, it is not clear where the secular ends and religion begins . . .

(Casanova 2006, 9, 12)

Lacking a disestablishment phase, America was both religious and secular at its inception. As a result, the two never had to battle for supremacy, perhaps best expressed by the separation between church and state implied in the United States Constitution. If Casanova is correct when he claims that it is "not clear where the secular ends and religion begins" in America, then the secular can effortlessly co-opt the religious and vice versa.

As expected, religion did not shrink or disappear in the United States as predicted by Berger and others. The 90 percent of Americans who still believe in God combined with a vocal persistence of religion in the public square evinces that religion does not seem to be going anywhere anytime soon. Yet the persistence of religion does not have an inverse effect on the secular—the secular mindset in America continues to assert itself boldly. By many accounts, *postsecularism* is the proper term used to describe the new ways that religion and the secular now commingle, both in the United States and in Europe.

Postsecularism sees religious ideologies existing alongside and relating to secular ideologies in novel ways. If the largely sacred world that dominated before secularization prioritized the religious, and the secular world that later asserted itself prioritized the secular, the postsecular prioritizes neither. Instead of the religious and the secular locked in a war, a postsecular context allows for the kind of relationship that effectively blurs the line between the two. For Talal Asad, this line is blurry because there is no sacred or secular essence to language or objects when you get right down to it. In his words:

> I take the view, as others have done, that the "religious" and the "secular" are not essentially fixed categories. However, I do not claim that if one stripped appearances one would see that some apparently secular institutions were really religious. I assume, on the contrary, that there is nothing essentially religious, nor any universal essence that defines "sacred language" or "sacred experience."
>
> (Asad 2003, 25)

What Asad means here is that there is nothing lurking underneath religious or secular language that is essentially religious. Likewise, peeling off the trappings of religious institutions will not disclose a secular essence below. And if there is nothing essential about sacred or secular things, then it becomes much more difficult to contain either in fixed categories or separate containers. With this, a new relationship between the sacred and secular opens up in a postsecular world, where the two do not exist in distinct silos. According to Robert Wuthnow, "the boundaries separating religious organizations from the wider culture have become more porous, thus permitting external influences to have a greater impact on religion than ever before and giving religious leaders greater opportunities to borrow from the wider culture" (Wuthnow 2007, 42–43). We argue that sports is one of these external influences.

But what are the mediums of exchange between the sacred and the secular in a postsecular world? How, exactly, do they communicate with each other? What, besides the failure of secularization to complete its process, permits and even encourages dialogue and mutual inter-penetration between religion and the secular? Sociologist Bryan Turner sees consumer culture and its tendency to commercialize everything it touches in order to sell to the masses as not only the vehicle that puts the religious and the secular in touch with each other, but also as that which blurs the difference between the two so that communi-cation can occur. According to Turner:

> If we look at religion in terms of a theory of media of exchange and communication, then democratization entails the disappear-ance of these ancient forms of sacredness and ineffability . . . Because communication comes from everywhere, we inhabit an information-saturated social world. In place of the ineffable character of the sacred realm, religion becomes fully available to the hoi polloi, because its message is made plain, simple, and direct through the commercialized media and popular culture . . . the idea of a necessary tension between religion and the world needs to be taken into account. Commercialization liquidates this tension, and democratization levels out the relationship between the sacred and the secular, producing a situation in which the world is flat.
>
> (Turner 2012, 139–140)

Because religion uses commercial techniques to compete in the marketplace of information, it already intersects with the secular simply by communicating in this way. Turner uses this fact to argue that the commercialization of religion and its accessibility to all serves to enact what Asad contends is already happening between the sacred and the secular—there is no necessary tension between the two. Moreover, the world is flattened, so to speak, when religion "lowers" itself from the heavens into the worldly realm of marketing. As Turner explains:

> Just as the secular market emphasizes choice for the secular consumer and the importance of niche marketing, so does the religious market. The American megachurch is modeled on the corporation in terms of architecture, culture, ambience, and outlook . . . The habitus of the modern adherent of deinstitutionalized religion is basically compatible with the lifestyles of a commercial world in which the driving force of the economy is domestic consumption. Megachurches have embraced the sales strategies of late capitalism in order to get their message out to the public.
>
> (Turner 2012, 140)

Hence, in a postsecular context, the authority of religion is maintained not by returning to an old-time religion, but by accommodating itself to secular ways of life.

Alternatively, in this flattened world of postsecularity, secular institutions now must relate to religion as they both operate in the same plane. For this to happen, secular institutions must understand themselves differently in relation to religion than was the case when science and the secular state pushed religion into the private realm (de Vries and Sullivan 2006, 3). Instead of a secular activity thinking of itself as superior to religion or as winning the cultural battle (because no battle was actually won), it must understand itself as coexisting with religion, and even at times cooperating with it in the pursuit of common goals. In fact, most scholars analyzing the postsecular are reluctant to locate postsecularity as a historical period that follows a secular epoch in the West because it "doesn't express a sudden increase in religiosity, after its epochal decrease, but rather a change in the mindset of those who, previously, felt justified in considering religions to be moribund" (Hans Joas in ibid., 2–3). The postsecular is more of an indicator of a new relationship between the sacred and the secular that secular institutions, in particular, are in need of recognizing.

Turner's "flat world" metaphor helps us make sense of the traffic-flow along the cultural web. And sports is, at least on the surface, a non-religious, secular activity that is thoroughly entrenched in the machinery of capitalism. Turner would echo William Baker's remarks that, "Religion and sport especially are joined at the altar of commercial interest" (Baker 2007, 4). And the primary means by which sports generates money is its ability to resonate with a mass audience or, in other words, be a major player in popular culture. According to Conrad Ostwalt, the high visibility of popular cultural items makes them particularly good secular partners to their religious counterparts. He writes of a different kind of flow along the cultural web in a postmodern (read postsecular) context:

> If the modern era promised the disappearance of religion through secularization, the postmodern era promises the increased visibility of religion, although not necessarily in traditional packages. Contemporary American culture witnesses secularization occurring in two directions: 1) the churches and religious organizations are becoming increasingly more attune to the secular environment, particularly to popular culture, and are in some cases trying to emulate it in the effort to remain relevant; 2) popular cultural forms, including literature, film, and music, are becoming increasingly more visible vehicles of religious images, symbols, and categories. These two directions of secularization demonstrate the blurred or malleable boundaries between religion and culture—the sacred and the secular—that define the relationship of religion and culture in the postmodern era.
>
> (Ostwalt 2003, 28–29)

The first direction he calls the "sacralization of the secular," and the second direction he calls the "secularization of the sacred." These phrases themselves convey how there is a web of interweaving cultural relations in the postsecular, late capitalist world. This is a world where sports can be "sacralized" and religion can be "secularized," and through these dual movements, the boundaries that used to contain and insulate religion and sports are crossed repeatedly.

Yet the crossing of boundaries or leaking of "porous boundaries" from one to the other can still allow each to retain its legitimacy as religion and sports, regardless of an ongoing desire to silo the two. The interaction between the sacred and secular does not mean that their identities are lost as such. They use each other to enrich themselves without undermining the other; they feed off each other rather than fight. This means, for example, that a sports bar can convert into a kind of modern temple where patrons show devotion by donning team jerseys and sidling up to their "altar" to watch the game. Here the secular is sacralized as religious undertones are at home in the most secular of environments. This doesn't mean that there is a conspiracy to hide religious elements in sports or that sports exploits religion. Nor is the competition between religion and sports, as is often presented in culture, a zero-sum game where an increase in Sunday football viewership means that religion loses if church attendance decreases. Instead, this simply means that religion and sports have an intimate and fruitful relationship.

The Cultural Approach to Religion and Sports

When we attempt to understand the relationship between religion and sports on the level of *culture*, we are departing from many of the typical paths scholars have followed to understand the relationship. To clarify our approach to the relationship, it is helpful to survey some of these other ways in which the relationship between religion and sports has been examined. There are five major trends in the academic treatment of sports and religion that fall largely along disciplinary lines. The first (not in order of importance) is the *historical* approach, which follows the sports/religion bond as a thread running from antiquity to the present. In this approach, the Olympic Games can be seen as enacting ancient religious rituals intended to appease the gods. Little distinction is drawn between the athletic activity and its religious origins, and modern manifestations of sports are culled for similar historical wellsprings.

This "origins meta-narrative" (an overarching story that helps explain what underlies many narratives found in history) is certainly useful in the attempt to understand some religious residues found in modern sports. It's not simply linking many separate stories together, but instead finding a commonality or cohesive way of explaining all of them at once. According to the historical approach, the origins of all sports are found to be religious. Using this meta-narrative, any question about the peculiarities or survivability of a specific sport is explained by locating its religious remnants or qualities. Often the notion of *play* in sports is classified as a kind of other-worldly activity that, like religion, transcends the chores of daily life. William Baker (2007) is a prominent advocate of this approach.

We find this approach insightful, but to some extent, a bit reductionist. Even though it is true that all major sports have long histories that have included religious elements, it would be difficult to argue, based on Asad's claim, that sports derives its *gravitas* and appeal exclusively from an underlying religious core. Sports is founded on religious beliefs and practices as much as on secular principles and institutions, especially in its current form. As Allen Guttmann claims:

> For most contemporary athletes, even for those who ask for divine assistance in the game, the contest is a secular event. The Sermon on the Mount does not interfere with hard blocking and determined tackling. Religion remains on the sidelines.
>
> (Guttmann 1978, 25)

The second approach is *sociological* in nature. What characterizes this approach is that it is a continuation of classical sociological thought, from Max Weber to Emile Durkheim and beyond, whereby social institutions, such as the family or a community, are examined in terms of their structures, values, and organization. For some sociologists, such as Steven Overman (2011), sports is one of these institutions that builds its structure on a religious foundation, knowingly or not. He draws on Max Weber's argument that seventeenth-century Calvinist theology sowed the seeds of later capitalistic development in Protestant communities. Or, to understand the rise of capitalism, one must unearth its religious roots. Hence, viewing the relationship between sports and religion in this way helps uncover some of the hidden rationale that guides and justifies the structure of organized sports. As Overman claims, "the ethos of American sport is best explained as a derivative of secularized Protestant values operating within the milieu of industrial (and now post-industrial) capitalism" as his focus is, "on the legacy of a religious ethic as the source of the prevailing spirit of sport" (Overman 2011, 16).

There is no doubt that organized sports has been influenced by institutionalized religion and that religious remnants are still present. Yet just because something is historically prior to something else does not mean that it caused it or, more importantly, that a causal link between religion and sports is the best way to understand their relationship. The local church that dates back to the sixteenth century, for example, is not necessarily the model for today's soccer team in the same town. Both are institutions and as such have structures and rules of conduct. But this parallel alone does not express a deeper indebtedness of soccer to Calvinism. Again, as with the historical approach, we try to avoid any perception that sports is exclusively or causally derived from religious institutions.

The third approach is *economic* in nature. The commercialization of sports in modern capitalism transforms it into another product that is bought and sold in the marketplace. From this economic perspective, sports is just like any other commodity whose value is measured in dollars and cents. More to the point, sports has no value to a mass audience outside of its market value; it can *only* be understood as a business. Three conclusions follow from this approach that involve the relationship between sports and religion. First, following this logic, both sports and religion are businesses based on how they run and on the amount of money they bring into their coffers. Second, both sports and religion serve as distractions from the real economic injustices that prevail in capitalism, according to William Morgan (1994), a proponent of this approach. And third, though both religion and sports share common ties to the prevailing economic culture, the services they provide are different. Paying for a sporting event is different from tithing. In sports, monetary payment brings entertainment value, while church offerings are charitable in nature. Can competitive sports be played for the pure love of the game? Can a church survive without focusing on the bottom line? In other words, can both institutions avoid participation in the marketplace?

As stated earlier, we certainly acknowledge that money plays a powerful role in religion and sports, and as cultural forms, they cannot avoid meeting up in the marketplace, for capitalism touches every facet of culture in some way. In addition, we come close to this approach by relying on Turner's contention that the commercialization of religion effectively blurs the line between the sacred and the secular. Having said this, despite the important role that capitalism plays in allowing the sacred and the secular to commingle today, religion is not related to sports *strictly* on the basis of their participation in the machinery of capitalism. That both are commercialized does not necessarily lead to the conclusion that religion and sports can *only* be understood as heavily commercialized institutions or compared to each other based on price as one would in a supermarket. Albanese's codes of living that sports transmits seem to transcend mere cash-value. Both religion and sports attempt to inculcate values such as honesty and justice through codes of living that, at least in principle, avoid being bought and sold to a mass audience. The packaging of these values does get caught up in the commercialization process, as we fully acknowledge throughout this book, but not necessarily the values themselves.

The fourth approach is *theological* insofar as sports is able to disclose religious truths. Religion and sports relate to each other in a kind of message–messenger relationship respectively. Greg Smith (2010), as an example of an author who takes this approach, predicates his argument on the claim that athletic ability is a gift from God. From here, sports is a means by which God relates to humanity through the gifts that God has given as well as a lens through which to see God's ways. Here, religion is not simply historically prior to or a sociological model for sports. Instead, religion is the foundation on which all human behavior, including athletic activity, depends. Sports is a way to glorify God and live out God's will, but seems to have no value apart from its ability to transmit theological truths. A softer version of theological approach can be found in John Sexton's *Baseball as a Road to God: Seeing Beyond the Game* where mystical elements of the game are said to percolate beneath the surface, giving the game its ultimate meaning, as the subtitle suggests (Sexton 2013). However, like our contention with the historical and sociological approach, when sports is made to be the handmaiden of religion, the new postsecular ways in which the sacred and secular intermingle are missed or ignored altogether. Neither religion nor sports escapes the clutches of culture, and therefore we cannot interpret the relationship between religion and sports as one that only points to transcendent truths—a status for both religion *and* sports that would inappropriately perch them above culture.

The fifth approach to the relation between sports and religion is *personal* and often *autobiographical*. Writing about sports and religion seems to invite authorial reflections of past experiences with sporting events and figures that tend to romanticize them. Their memories of sports heroes and events, while undoubtedly powerful and authentic, can exaggerate what actually happened. These authors tend to do hagiography rather than biography: Mickey Mantle is a baseball legend in every way possible only by overlooking his personal failures. Nostalgia for a purported pristine past encourages a kind of romanticism towards the world of sports, which, when abstracted from reality, results in these powerful personal experiences being more easily converted into religious ones. Religion and sports meet on the grounds of a similar feeling that both are, no doubt, able to generate. Michael Novak's *The Joy of Sports* and Harry Edwards' *Sociology of Sport* contain examples in which such an approach is taken (Edwards 1973; Novak 1994). On some level, it's impossible to be disengaged from one's personal experience when researching a topic, but on another, the personal isn't necessarily universal or profound. However weighty an experience or memory happens to be, this does not necessarily mean that it possesses religious content. True, most religious experiences are profound, but not all profound experiences are religious. Moreover, the move from romanticization to religion bypasses troublesome features of the latter— ones that must be included in any talk of the relationship between religion and sports.

The approach applied in our book is a *cultural* one. As far as we are concerned, it's not merely that both religion and sports are culturally mediated or that they are linked together in the cultural web. What interests us is the unique influence they have on each other that allows them to retain their differences while displaying a great deal of functional similarities. It is the seeing of sports and religion as cultural expressions (their language, their actions) that prevents putting one above another, as if that could be accomplished anymore. In other words, a cultural analysis of the relationship between religion and sports holds the promise of exposing the way they relate in a postsecular context.

To further distinguish our approach, it may be helpful to look at another way of using cultural expressions to get at the relationship between religion and sports that approximates ours, but conveys disparities that make a difference. Joseph Price, in the introduction to his *From Season to Season: Sports as American Religion*, supports the kind of relationship between sports and religion that corresponds to some of the developments brought on by postsecularism. According to Price:

> The contemporary tendency to connect athletic success and divine favor—or simply to blend the spirit of sporting competition with the fervor of evangelical piety—suggests that the convergence of sports and religion involves a kind of denigration of one or both, the profanation of the sacred or the diminution of sporting competition. However, the process of their modern mixing perhaps represents a reintegration of two sorts of rituals rather than a profanation of sacred rites.
>
> (Price 2001, 16)

Because one doesn't denigrate the other, "reintegration" is possible in contemporary culture. Here, both sports and religion seem to be relating as partners rather than competitors. But what will reintegration entail, and how is it to be understood?

Price puts forth five ways that religion and sports have historically interacted in order to answer this question. The first is called "religion and sports in conflict" (Ibid., 17). It is possible to argue that religion has nothing to do with sports and will combat it and other secular cultural forms when religious territory is encroached upon. This kind of relationship is reminiscent of the injunction attributed to Jesus in the synoptic gospels, which reads, "Render unto Caesar the things which are Caesar's, and unto God the things that are God's" (Matthew 22:21). Separation necessitates boundaries that, in turn, necessitate securing borders.

The second is called "sports commingling with religion" (Ibid., 21). This category is filled by Price with examples of sports and religion dabbling in each other's areas but never fully immersing in or rejecting the other. The reprimanding of sports figures for their immoral actions by religious authorities is constitutive though not exhaustive of this kind of relationship between religion and sports.

The third is labeled "religion conscripting sports" (Ibid., 23), where pastors and religious leaders utilize sports for their own purposes. They draw on the values of sports, such as dedicated athleticism, fair play, and sportsmanship, to legitimize certain religious principles. In this type of relationship, religion poaches on sports, as we saw in Paul's usage of the race as a metaphor, to make itself more culturally relevant as it translates the mundane into the profound.

The fourth is the flipside of the third: "sports co-opting religion" (Ibid., 31) where religion is used or co-opted by sports figures who employ religious language to legitimize or explain their athletic pursuits and/or success. Crediting God for a home run or qualifying a game as relatively unimportant in the bigger scheme of things are ways of taking athletic activity off of the field and dropping it onto a much grander stage. Either sports are amplified, as in the case of God and the home run, or relativized, as in the case of the game being unimportant when compared to religion.

Finally, Price asserts that "sports supplanting religion" (Ibid., 34) is perhaps the most important way to think about the relationship today. As sports gains in popularity and continues to reflect American values, it threatens to replace traditional religion as the vehicle for religious convictions and ways of life. Again, for Price, the increasing role of sports in the lives of Americans does not amount to the denigration of religion, as one trumpeting the secularization theory may argue. Instead, sports and its conspicuous place in American culture offer the opportunity for religion to express itself in different, perhaps even more significant ways than before.

Yet the kind of religion that is found in sports, according to Price, is that which relies on Mircea Eliade's concept of the *homo religious*. The human being is essentially religious, therefore sports will naturally reflect religion, even though it may take an investigation into the culture of sports to uncover it. Price argues that sports, like, "many forms of contemporary secular rituals manifest fundamental religious proclivities of human beings and reflect the sacred rites and myths of previous, religiously oriented cultures" (Ibid., 8). And then later, he remarks, "in several respects the fusion of sports and religion, especially during the latter portion of the twentieth century, represents the restoration of metaphysical and mystical impulses that generated or characterized early forms of play" (Ibid., 16–17). Here, once again, religion is antecedent to all other human activities, including athletic ones, because of its foundational nature. Despite overtures to a cultural analysis of the relationship between religion and sports that would see them both as unique but in a sense equal on the cultural web, Price uses culture to show that sports is essentially religious at the core. Perhaps without intending to do so, sports is denigrated on his reading.

We do not challenge the wording or contours of Price's categories insofar as the relationship between religion and sports has been and is currently being expressed in all of these ways. Though his use of culture to understand the relationship corresponds to our own approach, Price seems to have a different goal in mind. Because religion is primary for Price, even if sports supplants religion on the cultural front, the *homo religiosus* will merely use sports to satisfy its deep-seated and permanent religious needs, notwithstanding Asad's claim to the contrary. Whether they are fighting, commingling, co-opting, or supplanting, sports and religion will end up playing a kind of shell game in which the "ball" is always religion.

When looking at the relationship between religion and sports on the level of its cultural expression through a postsecular lens, as we do in this book, it will be apparent that sports does not *replace* religion nor is it merely "religion in disguise." Rather, sports can *displace* the exclusive centrality of religious institutions as the *only* backdrop for political and moral integrity. Sports does so by engaging themes and concepts historically reserved for religious use and then transmits the meaning of these in more culturally relevant ways than religion can currently do. The notion of displacement as opposed to replacement is a theoretical commitment that can be found in both postmodernist and postsecularist thought. Here, there is an admission that something new in the relationship between the sacred and the secular might be happening and that this novelty fits into an established framework without thereby dismantling, subsuming, or replacing that framework. The established framework that houses these religious themes and concepts is still religion. If a term such as "Hail Mary" is used in football, we can be sure that its religious sources help to frame its meaning and use in a sports context. In this manner, sports highlights the advantages and drawbacks of the use of religious terminology without necessarily superseding it. The notion of displacement means that the integrity of both remains intact. Think of the Archimedean principle of water displacement in a bathtub: when an object is inserted, the water level rises; it is displaced. But water doesn't necessarily overflow, nor is it somehow replaced by the object.

Instead of having to engage in a full-fledged study of the religious notion of redemption, for example, one can still grasp the contemporary meaning of the concept when considering, say, the desire of Pete Rose to get into the baseball Hall of Fame after being accused of gambling on games in which he was a participant. Entrance into the Hall of Fame can constitute Rose's redemption. Sports, in this case, displaces religion as the primary carrier of meaning, but redemption in sports resonates only because its religious mirror-image may have been already accepted in theological terms by society at large. The religious content of redemption neither disappears nor or is replaced when religion and sports come together around this concept. The resonance of the religious component of redemption is not due to religion being superior, prior, or sacred in comparison to sports. Rather, it's because of its *familiarity*. Religious images and ideals have been culturally available in more pronounced and explicit fashion over the centuries, and therefore have been used in a host of other non-religious contexts with more and more ease. Sports just happens to be a particularly influential, non-religious context in American culture today.

Each chapter of our book focuses on a singular concept, such as redemption, that draws out particular cultural expressions in both sports and religion (primarily as expressed in the Bible). Each concept will be described both historically and theoretically, so as to provide the means to examine multiple interpretations in both religion and sports in four sections found in each chapter. Section 1 of each chapter looks at the biblical expression of the chosen concept and its classic Western religious commentary. Section 2 chronicles the use of the concept in sports by athletes and fans alike. Section 3 contextualizes the concept in the contemporary American religious landscape with special attention paid to the analyses of social theorists. And finally, section 4 draws on insights from the previous three sections in order to disclose how sports and religion come together around the concept in contrast to the use of the concept in contemporary cultural debates and controversies.

It should be noted that we focus on the Bible not because it holds elevated significance above and beyond other religious or non-religious texts, but rather because it happens to be the predominant source for religious and moral discussion in American culture, including sports. However, when citing biblical passages, we refrain from delving into nuanced debates among biblical scholars about the "correct meaning" of these passages. We do this because our interest is in the way that the wider, contemporary culture uncritically appropriates these passages in relation to the concept that we also find in sports.

For example, when discussing the concept of "belief" in Chapter 1, we will illustrate how it has been applied by athletes, fans, and religious leaders. It will become evident that, though different on some levels, there are parallels that demonstrate the ongoing conversation, perhaps implicit more than explicit, between all of them. Athletes and congregants alike put their faith in the unknown, whether in the hoped-for outcome of the game or in the afterlife. Using sports stories and biblical vignettes, which are cultural expressions themselves, we will hopefully demonstrate that sports functions *like* religion, sports *borrows* the language of religion, and an *alternative* cultural environment in which to understand the relationship between religion and sports will materialize.

In terms of religion, this means that religion as such has never ceased to exist, nor does it need to cease to exist in order for secular activities to flourish. In terms of sports, this means that sports continues to be a cultural expression of meaningful concepts and a carrier of codes of behavior that are transmitted from one generation to another, regardless of religion. In other words, there is *no contest* between the two sets of cultural practices. In their differences, the public can find interesting points of contact and shared commitments to the good life, in spite of the media's presentations to the contrary. We approach the relationship between sports and religion not in order to convert sports into a new religion or to classify it as a purely secular activity. What will become clear in our book is that sports is religious in some sense and that knowledge of religion is helpful in explaining tragedies and triumphs that occur in sports on a regular basis. Likewise, religion is an athletic activity in some sense, and knowledge of sports is helpful in explaining tragedies and triumphs in one's religious life. It's no longer a contest between sports and religion or sports *versus* religion, but an accommodation in the cultural web that includes sports *and* religion.

1

BELIEF

From broadcaster Al Michaels' famous line at the end of the United States hockey team's improbable victory over the Soviet Union in the 1980 Olympics, "Do you believe in miracles?," to Paul's claim that belief in the miracle of Jesus' resurrection is sufficient for salvation, the concept of belief is used in both sports and religion quite frequently and with ease. In both of these cases, the term "belief" or "believe" puts a potential believer in relation to something that may be unbelievable in normal daily life: a miracle. A highly improbable victory in a sports game is more easily believed than a bodily resurrection from the dead, though for some, to believe in the historical event of Jesus' resurrection is not difficult at all. It is simply an essential article of faith within Christianity. And for yet another group, belief in any miracle is impossible. The reason for these varying ways of relating to a miracle, if they occur at all, is that there are several different kinds of belief.

A sports "miracle" may not entail a suspension of laws of nature but may be merely an event that exceeds any reasonable expectations or probability. Hence, in sports, belief may be needed to trust that the highly doubtful will happen or that it just did happen when it was "beyond belief" before and during the game. And on a more mundane level, belief is what holds together the unfolding of events from the present to the future. To some extent, we must believe that the plane that we are on will land safely because we don't know for a fact that it will, though the chances are great that all will be well.

If we define a belief as what we hold to be true without reliable empirical or observed evidence, then a belief, by definition, does not guarantee that what we believe in is, in fact, true. We may believe that the statement, "my car will start in the morning" is true, but we certainly do not *know* if it will start—we *believe* that it will based on our past experiences of reliably starting our car. Here and as it is in most philosophical treatments of the concept of belief, belief is contrasted with knowledge. I know that $2 + 2 = 4$, but I can only believe that I will pass the upcoming math exam. Or after the exam, I know that I passed because the grade reads 82. It would be strange to say that I believe I received an 82 on the exam after I saw the grade —I now know it to be the case. Despite various types of belief that we all practice in our daily lives, the fact that sports and religion draw on such a concept suggests that the interplay between belief and knowledge informs its use in both discourses.

Belief in the Bible

Belief is required in religion. Because religions typically deal with notions of God, divine reality, revelation, miracles, or an afterlife that are rarely experienced through any of the five senses, religious adherents are often asked to *believe* that these entities exist and that propositions about them are true. Hindus believe that Atman (one's soul) is the same thing as Brahman (divine reality) without *knowing* for certain that this is true. Buddhists believe that their own suffering can end without knowing that it will. And Muslims believe that Muhammad received Allah's revelation without any personal eyewitness evidence that this actually happened. Indeed, creeds, which stand as the foundation of many of the world religions, derive from the Latin *credo* meaning, "I believe." Belief in all of these religions is not based on knowledge of the claim made even though the belief may be incredibly strong.

Another word used to express belief within religion, especially in Jewish and Christian traditions, is faith. Faith, though, is different from the mere belief that God exists or that divine action occurred in the world. Faith in God involves a relationship with the divine—trusting God, loving God, fearing God—so that one has faith *in* God instead of merely believing that God is there—though the belief that God exists is certainly a prerequisite for having faith in God. For instance, when God tells Abraham in the book of Genesis Chapter 22 to go up on a mountain and sacrifice his son Isaac, Abraham did not know (perhaps he believed) that God was bluffing. As the story recounts, he believed that it was God talking to him without seeing God. But more importantly, Abraham had faith in a God that would not lead him astray. A prior commitment to God (faith) is necessary in order for doubts to be overcome. But Abraham also had to believe that it was God speaking to him in order to place his faith in this God. Abraham is honored by Jews, Christians, and Muslims alike for his faith in the God who ultimately has his best interests at heart despite appearances to the contrary. It is not Abraham's certain, indubitable knowledge that God would spare Isaac, but his faith in a trustworthy God that pushes him to obey.

Similarly, given every reason to lose his faith in God (elimination of all of his possessions and offspring and infliction with boils), the character of Job from the Bible continues to believe that God's actions are legitimate (whether or not they are in reality) and beneficial. And in the Christian scriptures, Paul continually proclaims to those who were not eyewitnesses to Jesus' life and death that belief in the effectiveness and sufficiency of God's sacrifice of a son is all that is needed to be put into a right standing before God. As Paul writes in his letter to the Galatians, "we have come to believe in Christ Jesus, so that we might be justified by faith in Christ" (Galatians 2:16, NRSV). Again, many of those listening to Paul 2,000 years ago or reading Paul today *believe* that they can arrive at the truth of such a proposition about God and salvation through faith.

In all of these cases, religious belief and/or faith provides the crucial bridge that connects finite humans to an infinite divine being. Believers are oriented to divine truth despite, or perhaps because of, the fact that the object of faith or the events that are believed in remain ultimately inaccessible to the senses. For religious thinkers over the centuries, the unknowability of divine truths has not meant that religious belief or faith is somehow a lesser or insufficient way to understand certain truths, though. In other words, belief may actually act as a *better* way of accessing the truth about the world than mere knowledge in some cases. As Jesus said to Thomas, the disciple that doubted that the resurrected Christ was standing in front of him, "Have you believed because you have seen me? Blessed are those who have not seen and yet have come *to believe*" (John 20:29, NRSV, italics added). Jesus seems to value the kind of belief that does not have empirical evidence to support it over that which does.

Similarly, Augustine (354–430 C.E.), an early and influential Christian theologian, makes faith the foundation for any understanding of the world. For him, the use of reason to figure out the world is based on the ability given to humans by way of their faith in God to fully understand the world. Once faith is in place, reason is a useful human tool—God-given, of course—to fully discover the mysteries of God's creation. "Faith seeking understanding" sums up his stance on the relationship between belief in God and reason. Faith in the God who created and ordered the world must precede any rational understanding of it. Otherwise, the world that we claim to understand has a shaky, misplaced, human-centered foundation.

The medieval Catholic theologian Thomas Aquinas (1225–1274) takes a slightly different stance than Augustine by putting faith and reason more or less on equal footing: both are gifts from God that furnish us with the ability to comprehend God's creation. Creation is both material and spiritual and is revealed to us by God; however, we need different lenses to see each of these qualities. We can observe the material world and use our reason to figure out that, say, God must have created the universe because something cannot be created out of nothing or that God is the Creator who was not created. But reason alone is limited when it comes to understanding the revelation of spiritual truth contained in the Bible that resists logical explanation. Claims of the Bible that Jesus is God's son or that the soul lives on after death are not accessible through observation or made coherent through reason. It is faith in God and in the truth of God's word that confirms these claims, for Aquinas. Therefore, faith and reason have separate duties but are charged with achieving a similar goal: that of understanding the ways in which God has revealed Godself to us.

Dutch philosopher Baruch (Benedict de) Spinoza (1632–1677) provides an unusual bridge between humans and God that fashions yet another relationship between belief and reason. Instead of drawing directly on the Bible, he offers a notion of nature as the embodiment and expression of the divine such that God *is* nature. Instead of belief and knowledge of the world operating separately and then relating to each other in a hierarchy (Augustine) or on parallel tracks (Aquinas), Spinoza brings the two together into one coherent package. Closing the distance between God and nature means that the distance between faith in God and the world is likewise closed. This way of thinking about belief or faith becomes more materialistic rather than transcendental or spiritual. For Spinoza, faith is not simply a way of thinking or accessing truth, but a way of acting. Acting in virtue towards other people and towards the natural world around us constitutes being faithful to God. In this way, moral action is an expression as much as a means to strengthen belief—the two are completely dependent on each other.

The Danish philosopher Søren Kierkegaard (1813–1855), like Aquinas, relies on reason to accomplish much in furthering our understanding of the world. Yet reason for Kierkegaard is used as an instrument to reveal its own limitations when attempting to comprehend Christ's incarnation. This event (the infinite God entering finite time and space in the person of Jesus) is a paradox that we cannot unravel with our reason. The only way to access the truth of the incarnation is to make a "leap of faith" that is not informed by reason at all. Reason is helpful in revealing our limitations, but when attempting to push through these limits, the only option is a blind leap into unknown territory. Then, and only then, for Kierkegaard, can we enjoy the radical saving power of Jesus Christ.

One of the contributions of Martin Luther (1483–1546) was to initiate the shift from social, organized faith to individual, personal belief. In contrast with the Catholic Church that elevated its own role in the lives of congregants at that time, Luther held that every individual can learn about God and salvation through the reading of the Bible alone.

By the nineteenth century, Americans were displaying a wide variety of expressions of religious belief, as noted by William James (1842–1910) who cited a "variety of religious experiences" to talk about religion in general. The upshot was the legitimization of many different paths to ultimate truth; some closely tied to the latest scientific developments of the time and some spiritual to the point of possessing minimal adherence to the Bible. In this kind of pluralistic environment, the proliferation of different modes of religious belief makes sense: you can choose what church to join based on your own set of beliefs, and expect that your beliefs will be reflected in the mission of your chosen church. Otherwise, the search can continue for a religious community that reflects your beliefs.

Despite the growing variety of religious or spiritual beliefs in America, all share the common function of orienting the believer to that mystery that is beyond the reach of the five senses. Religion, whether expressed in the Bible or elsewhere, is nothing if not that which involves objects and realities beyond the immanent world that we see and touch. Otherwise, religion would be science. Knowledge of these transcendent, ethereal truths is not feasible, but belief in them is. It is for this reason that belief, while perhaps denigrated in the scientific world, is absolutely necessary in religious ones.

Belief in Sports

Unlike with religion, beliefs have a difficult time fitting into the sports world. If all a player has is the belief that she is a good athlete, until her athleticism is proven on the field, the value of that belief alone remains suspect. Similarly, if a sports fan believes that Muhammad Ali was the greatest boxer of all time, that belief will be difficult to hold if statistics that measure Ali's success in the ring do not back up such a belief. And worse, if an athlete believes him or herself to be greater than what the statistics reveal, those stats will have to improve for the belief to be sustained. Baltimore Ravens quarterback, Joe Flacco, claimed that he believed that he was the best quarterback in the NFL while finishing eighteenth in the 2011 season in quarterback rating. His comments provoked widespread incredulity from fans and media alike who either wanted him to take his statement back or back it up with better play on the field the next season. In all of these cases, unlike religious belief, the legitimacy of a "sports belief" is more heavily tied to observed and measurable performance. Therefore, the kind of belief needed in sports requires a completely different set of conditions to work when compared to religion.

This is not to say that beliefs have not played a major role in sports historically or that they have disappeared altogether. Athletes consistently value the belief in their ability, which often leads to their determination to bring that ability to the surface. Likewise, fans trot out slogans such as, "You gotta believe!" when the odds are against their team. They even helped adopt Journey's "Don't Stop Believin'" as the official song for the Chicago White Sox during their 2004 World Series run. So, how should we think of belief when it involves sports? How does belief relate to sports when one team's play on the field, court, or ice often trumps the earnest beliefs of the opposing team? Or what happens to beliefs in the sports world when performance that is measured with empirical data is valued over the mere belief that one is a superior performer?

In ancient Greece, Olympians performed sacrifices of animals at once to please the gods *and* receive a blessing that could assure victory. Roman gladiators entered the arena with their dominant foot forward, believing that it would safeguard them from defeat in the lion's den. In many cases from ancient history, participants held the belief that these pregame rituals would affect the game itself. Back then, the actions of the gods and humans converged seamlessly, making the belief correspond with material events without tension. Today, however, pregame rituals that do not involve practice or seem to be directly related to the task at hand may be seen as remnants of these ancient practices, but they are not held to bear on the outcome of the game quite as easily as they once did.

Despite the improbability that devout prayer helps basketballs go in the basket, this hasn't stopped today's athletes and fans from hedging their bets with the supernatural. If a pregame prayer or ritual *may* help, why not use it? And when these kinds of activities take place, there must be a belief in some force that stands above but can affect the game, however vague or insincere that belief is. Yet religion is largely kept on the sidelines in sports discourse when it is expressed through the belief in the efficacy of certain pregame rituals. Hence, those kinds of beliefs are often given the derogatory label, "superstitions."

Famous superstitions in sports include Michael Jordan wearing his college game shorts under his pro uniform for every basketball game that he played for the Chicago Bulls. Baseball Hall of Famer Wade Boggs ate chicken before each game of his long career. Boggs did so because he had success the first several times after performing this ritual. And Sidney Crosby of hockey's Pittsburgh Penguins never talks to his mother on the phone the day of a game. Every time in the past that he talked to her on a game day, he got injured. Similarly, fans routinely wear their lucky jersey and watch the big game at the same bar or restaurant with the hope that their clothing and the location have the power to bring about a repeat performance. Rally caps (flipped under baseball caps) are worn by fans in the late innings of baseball games to spur their team to a comeback victory. Some rituals are overtly religious and less likely to be thought of as superstitious. Ivan "Pudge" Rodriguez, baseball catcher, would bless himself with his right hand over his chest before every pitch. And National Basketball Association player Jeremy Lin performs an elaborate, religiously significant handshake with a teammate before each basketball game.

Some religious rituals that are observed in the midst of sports but are not meant to bring about some future event may only be tangential to the action on the field. These involve the faith of the athlete rather than belief. Jewish pitcher Sandy Koufax declined to pitch in the first game of the 1965 World Series because it fell on the holiday of Yom Kippur, and Mahmoud Abdul-Rauf refused to stand with his Denver Nuggets teammates during a pregame national anthem because of his interpretation of his Islamic beliefs. These actions are motivated by strong religious beliefs and operate within a faith, but they just happen to intersect with sports rather than serve as a part of the game.

It is just as difficult to prove whether some of these superstitious actions have any bearing on performance as it is to gauge the strength of the belief in the efficacy of these rituals. In all likelihood, Crosby doesn't seriously believe that talking to his mother will actually cause injury on the ice any more than Boggs believes that eating chicken before a game makes him hit better. Then why continue these rituals if they do not really cause good play? Skepticism aside, there still must be a belief, however small, that either these rituals have some magical power or that some unknown force is connecting radically different events. Otherwise, these odd rituals would be replaced with more logical ones, such as watching game tape. Jordan would likely give credit to his hard work for his success and, despite his ritual action, admit that wearing an extra pair of shorts is irrelevant to his success. Perhaps it is the comfort of a routine that keeps these rituals alive, but they are kept alive nonetheless.

Because fans have much less or, more likely, no control over their team's fate, they may have a greater need to call on spiritual forces to bridge the gap between their wants and the results of the game. Players and coaches have recourse to their own, more intimate explanations for wins and losses—they know why the game turned out the way it did because they were involved directly in it. And while fans can see what happened on the field too, the action is always at arm's length. The belief in and use of a "curse" to explain (and therefore control, to a degree) historic stretches of losing seasons is one way to mitigate the pain. The curses that are believed to have plagued baseball's Boston Red Sox and the Chicago Cubs (we will discuss the latter's curse in Chapter 3 in more detail) are the most prominent. The Red Sox had won five of the first fifteen World Series, the last in 1918, when they traded Babe "The Bambino" Ruth to the relatively lackluster New York Yankees in 1920. The Red Sox then went on an 86-year championship drought while the Yankees won twenty-six championships in that same time period. The Red Sox got close to winning several times throughout this period but always came up short, often because of implausible and downright unthinkable occurrences on the field. The unlikelihood of any team going that long without a trophy led some fans to attribute this not to unlucky bounces or simply to poor play but to the "Curse of the Bambino." The Red Sox finally broke the curse (what supernatural force helped break it is anyone's guess) by beating the Yankees on their way to winning the 2004 World Series.

Belief in a curse is a last resort for fans when the logic that typically guides the understanding of wins and losses breaks down time and time again. Stadiums can be cursed or blessed for some teams—it was rumored that Anaheim Stadium was built on top of a Native American burial ground, and the Angels paid the price by losing close games. The colors of uniforms are believed to be unlucky or cursed to a degree—Tiger Woods always wears red on the final day of a golf tournament, and the Dallas Cowboys will only wear white at home. Athletes who appear on the cover of the magazine *Sports Illustrated*, it is believed, are cursed to fail. For instance, Pat O'Connor, after appearing on the cover in 1958, died four days later on the first lap of the Indianapolis 500. And in 2003, the Oregon Ducks football team was placed on the cover after starting 4–0 and upsetting Michigan. They lost their next four games. Finally, the "Madden Curse" is believed to saddle athletes who grace the cover of the John Madden football video game box with a bad season. For one of the many examples that seem to support the curse, after Donovan McNabb's appearance on the 2006 cover, he tore the ACL in his right knee, ending his season.

One unique aspect of sports is that the outcome of a game or the final standings at the end of the season is never known at the start, unlike a book or a movie that has scripted endings. This open-ended, uncertain aspect of sports disallows *knowledge* of the ending as it invites *belief*. However, as these above examples all illustrate, there are different kinds and levels of beliefs in sports. Not only is there a difference in the beliefs of players, coaches, owners, fans, and media commentators, there is a different degree of belief for all of them. Some beliefs are unjustifiable in a scientific sense—they lack the empirical evidence of repeated attempts that warrant such a belief and are therefore deemed superstitious. Yet there are other beliefs that are more reasonable to uphold—enough of the same incident occurring over and over may allow for a justification for the belief that something beyond the field of play is involved in perpetuating the streak, both good and bad ones.

As regards the different degrees of belief in sports, it is easier to believe that your team will win the division when it has a sizable lead with a month to go. It is more difficult to believe (even when it is still statistically possible) that the last-place team will catch the leader with only a limited number of games left to play. Similarly, it takes more faith to maintain that a historic loser will somehow win this year or that a rookie will hit the winning shot. At the beginning of each season, because all teams start 0–0, the belief that one's team has a shot to win it all *should* be held equally by fans of all teams participating.

The reality, though, is that some teams have a head start, which can play a significant role in altering the belief in a team's chances. For example, Major League Baseball has no firm limit on what teams can spend on player salaries each year, which creates vast disparities in the talent that teams are allowed to procure. Teams that are unable or unwilling to spend a lot of money are at a severe disadvantage before the opening day first pitch is thrown. Fans of the small-market Kansas City Royals, for example, can only *believe* that they can win the World Series because the quality of players their owner has been willing to buy is far lower than most other teams. Alternatively, New York Yankee fans, knowing that their owner spends the most of any team each year on player salaries and stadium facilities, have a much more reasonable belief based on their *knowledge* of the empirical data that they will win it all.

Just as fans attempt to bolster their beliefs with evidence when they can, so do players. Ability and talent take top-level athletes just so far; all who make it to the pros are talented enough. It is the belief in one's own ability, even against all odds, that supplements and even feeds the talent that is already there. Rod Carew, Hall of Fame baseball player, once said:

> Do you believe you're a starter or a benchwarmer? Do you believe you're an all-star or an also-ran? When you've learned to shut off outside influences and believe in yourself, there's no telling how good a player you can be.

New York Giants football coach, Tom Coughlin, about overcoming incredible odds by winning the 2007 Super Bowl was quoted as saying:

> We knew nobody was giving us a shot, but we always believed in ourselves. . . . We never really cared what other people outside of those guys in that locker room or our owners or our coaching staff has said anyway.

Virginia Commonwealth University basketball coach, Shaka Smart said, after his small school knocked off powerhouse Connecticut to make it to the Final Four:

> Once again we felt like nobody really thought we could win going into this game. Our guys have done a phenomenal job of putting all the doubters aside, all the people that didn't believe in us, and going out to do their job.

In all of these cases, belief helps insulate the mind from doubt, which can affect the body's ability to do what the mind tells it.

Unlike in religion, belief in sports is not as central to the practice, though it is there. Talent on the field and the statistics that record such talent hold the *real* authority in the minds of athletes and fans alike. However, we see that despite its relative lack of authority in sports discourse, belief in superstitious rituals, curses, long odds, and one's own ability to beat those odds continues to play a major role in the way we think about sports. It is in this sense that sports and religion may not be as far apart as the skeptic wants to believe.

Belief and Religion Today

With the capacity of science to tell us much about the world we live in today, the belief, even knowledge, that God dictates the events of the world has been severely challenged over the last several centuries. No longer is the belief that God cures disease or causes hurricanes publicly endorsed or even widely held by religious people—we now have reliable "secular" explanations for both types of events. Yet, perhaps surprisingly, faith in God has not diminished in any substantial way in the United States. According to a 2011 Gallup Poll, 92 percent of Americans said they believed in God, and even more surprisingly, a 2009 Gallup Poll showed that only 39 percent of Americans believe in the theory of evolution. Clearly, religion has not lost its cache in contemporary American culture despite the encroachment of scientific thinking into territory previously occupied by religion.

Today we often hear about religion being at odds with science. Religion is based on faith; science on reason. Either you believe in creationism—the literal biblical narrative of God's creation of the universe 6,000 years ago—or in evolution—Charles Darwin's (1809–1882) theory of how humans evolved from more primitive species over millions of years. It seems that one cannot maintain both ways of thinking about the origins of the universe and humanity simultaneously. There have been attempts to complement scientific discovery with faith, though. Some argue that evolution can coexist with a creator God if evolution is considered the product of intelligent design. Others continue to argue that the evidence, both biblical and empirical, points to a creator, while the evidence for evolution is open to doubt and refutation. Still others mock any attempt to explain the world using the Bible because the workings of nature have nothing to do with what some consider Holy Scripture—science concerns nature; religion, the supernatural.

What is at stake in these contemporary debates is the status of certain sacred texts. For some, every word of the Bible comes from God; it's divine even when written by humans. Others suggest that the Bible is divinely inspired and that it contains God's Word, though not every part of the book is without error. This is the view that the Bible is divinely inspired, but not necessarily divinely written. Still others claim that the Bible is allegorical or metaphorical. The world took millions of years to be created, so when Genesis describes six days of creation, it's not literal but metaphorical—it actually took a long time to create the world and the Bible conveys this in words that figuratively represent the truth. Any one of these three ways of seeing the relationship between religion and science through the Bible requires a level of belief in that which transcends what appears to us in nature. Yet it should also be clear that the intensity of that belief has been altered significantly by the successes of science in explaining the world. Even the literalist interpretation, which is a movement that began in America only in the late nineteenth century, is a reaction to the challenge of evolutionary theory, but one that requires incredible faith in the face of the mounting evidence to the contrary.

However, philosopher Charles Taylor, in good postsecularist fashion, does not argue that an increase in the trusting of science or reason necessarily causes a decrease or even elimination of religious belief in a society. What characterizes our current age is the witnessing of a shift in the *kinds* of beliefs that we may now hold and even what it means to believe anything at all. He writes:

The shift to secularity in this sense consists, among other things, of a move from a society where belief in God is unchallenged and indeed, unproblematic, to one in which it is understood to be one option among others, and frequently not the easiest to embrace.

(Taylor 2007, 3)

The challenges to the belief in God posed by science and other secular institutions during a process of secularization left religious belief as one option among others, "exclusive humanism" being the main one, instead of standing alone as the *only* option, as it enjoyed before. Further, "unbelief has become for many the major default option" or the preferred option over the religious one.

The key for Taylor is that to assert that belief in God is merely an *option* in the West today means two primary things. One, "it may be hard to sustain one's faith" in the kind of environment that puts forth attractive alternatives to religious belief. But two, and more importantly, this new age still holds open the possibility for paths to transcendence that are needed by some to make sense of their lives. Yes, we can no longer return to a "naïve acknowledgment of the transcendent, or of goals or claims which go beyond human flourishing" (Ibid., 21). But in opposition to secularization theorists who predicted the end of religion, Taylor doesn't "see the cogency of the supposed arguments from, say, the finding of Darwin to the alleged refutations of religion" (Ibid., 4). The desire for human flourishing may still be able to tap (in fact for Taylor, they must tap) some notion of the transcendent that the scientific worldview simply cannot provide.

Indeed, scientists themselves display a level of faith in their theories and experiments. While scientific theories always rise and fall on the empirical evidence that supports or refutes them, no scientist in advance *knows* with certainty whether her experiment will work. She must *believe* that it will work so that her hypothesis can be trusted and the experiment can be carried out. Absent this belief, no longitudinal study would ever get off the ground nor have the momentum to cross the finish line. William James once wrote, "A chemist finds a hypothesis live enough to spend a year in its verification: he believes in it to that extent" (James 1956, 4). Therefore, belief, which we supposedly resort to when knowledge is not possible, seems to play a role in scientific inquiry and resolution. The boundaries separating religion and science may be more porous than commonly thought along the lines of what must be believed.

Belief in Religion and Sports

On one level, religion and sports interact with each other, based on the fact that beliefs are needed in both domains. As we have seen, the concept of belief is central to religion, but it is usually marginalized in sports. But what happens when sports meets religion around the issue of belief? Belief in curses, magic, or that God cares about the outcome of a sports game is commonly thought to be superstitious, self-serving, or theologically shallow. *New York Times* columnist David Brooks conveys this sentiment when he writes:

> Ascent in the sports universe is a straight shot. You set your goal, and you climb toward greatness. But ascent in the religious universe often proceeds by a series of inversions: You have to be willing to lose yourself in order to find yourself; to gain everything you have to be willing to give up everything; the last shall be first; it's not about you . . . Sports history is littered with odd quotations from people who try to reconcile their love of sport with their religious creed—and fail.

(Brooks 2012)

They fail if, like Brooks, one holds that religion and sports are radically different from and at odds with each other. But is Brooks correct? Despite some obvious differences between the belief statements in religion and in sports, a careful examination of their cultural expression shows a surprising number of similarities.

Faith, as expressed in religion and sports, can take several forms. Some, such as tennis star sisters Venus and Serena Williams, will talk about their convictions as Jehovah's Witnesses when asked by the media, but prefer to let their moral actions convey their beliefs and their play on the court speak for itself. Others, such as former football player

Reggie White, profess their belief that God is directly affecting play on the field and dictating for which team they will play. Somewhere in between stands Tim Tebow (whose story we mentioned in the Introduction), because he is both a believer and a football player who has won some unbelievable games.

There have been many reasons that pundits have given for the public's fascination with Tebow. *New Yorker*'s Reeves Weideman traces it to Tebow's unpredictability. He "is a loose cannon, capable of greatness and futility in equal measure, and in quick succession" (Weideman 2011). Kevin Craft of *The Atlantic* also sees contrasts working in Tebow but puts them on a bigger stage: "he is a serious young man in a silly adult world. He is an irony-free individual who seems uninterested in developing an athletic persona based upon rehearsed machismo or wink-wink self-awareness" (Craft 2011). Pop culture writer Chuck Klosterman sees Tebow's power as a kind of magic act that we cannot figure out:

> [Tebow] makes blind faith a viable option. His faith in God, his followers' faith in him—it all defies modernity. This is why people care so much. He is making people wonder if they should try to believe things they don't actually believe.
>
> (Klosterman 2011)

Are Tebow's beliefs and his ability to instill similar beliefs in fans beyond superstition? Does he embody a new way to convey religious commitment in the modern world? Or perhaps watching Tebow win games provokes a profound theological question, as Carter Turner suggests: "People are watching because for many, his games are about whether or not a God exists who intervenes in human history—even in the mundane, like football." And finally, Ross Douthat of the *New York Times* credits Tebow's character with the cause for the fascination. "It's because his conduct—kind, charitable, chaste, guileless—seems to actually vindicate his claim to be in possession of a life-altering truth" (Douthat 2012).

Culturally, as we have seen in the previous section, we have developed more subtle ways of thinking about and expressing our beliefs. Just as some Christians can live with scientific knowledge and its authority in a postsecular world, so can some of them live with beliefs expressed by athletes without threat to their own faith. The issue before us is no longer the choice between two or more sets of beliefs, but how they inform each other. Douthat proposes three types of people reacting to Tebow that may help us to see this more clearly. As he says:

> The sophisticated football fan will tell you that Tebow is a bad-to-mediocre quarterback with a few unusual skills who rode a lucky streak to undeserved fame; the rest is just the standard media fantasy about "intangibles" and "grit" dressed up with spirituality.
>
> (Ibid.)

Religion and sports should be kept apart, for the sophisticated fan. For when faith and sports unite, actual athletic ability or achievement gets too easily confused with sheer luck. Douthat continues:

> [T]he sophisticated atheist will inform you that in a vast and complicated cosmos, there will inevitably be temporary patterns that give the *appearance* of some divine design. But it would be even more ridiculous for a secular-minded football fan to root against Tebow than for a religious fan to root for him: in a godless, random universe, failure is no more metaphysically significant than success.
>
> (Ibid.)

This approach concedes that it looks like something supernatural may be happening with Tebow and the Broncos. But like the opinion of the sophisticated football fan, when it is believed that play on the field is endowed with religious significance, patterns are attributed to a God that aren't really there. Douthat's third type of respondent to Tebow, the sophisticated Christian, "may be a little embarrassed by the whole Tebow business. A sophisticate's God doesn't care about trivia like who wins football games. A sophisticate's theology doesn't depend on what some muscle head does with the pigskin" (Ibid.).

Recall that religious belief has historically been pitted against knowledge of the world as a means of acquiring truth. Beliefs that circulate in sports are always battling physical talent and stubborn statistics for an explanation of almost impossible events that happen during games. Both religion and sports beliefs have a common function: to transcend what is observed in order to access that which is not observed. This transcendence is meant to reach the truth, whether about God or that intangible reason that success on the field occurred. What remains different, though, no matter how similar the language involving beliefs is, is that once a team wins or loses, once an athlete breaks a record, there is no room for doubt. While in religion, belief remains so crucial because no amount of empirical evidence may ever undermine the faith of the believer. What has fascinated cultural commentators is the fact that this difference seems to have been lost. This is where the confusion and fascination come together as regards religious belief and sports. Concerning Tim Tebow, Klosterman writes, "the issue driving this whole 'Tebow Thing,' is the matter of faith. It's the ongoing choice between embracing a warm feeling that makes no sense or a cold pragmatism that's probably true" (Klosterman 2011).

The choice for many contemporary commentators seems to be between keeping sports a predictable contest and turning it into something more than it is. For us, this is a false dichotomy. Instead of thinking of sports becoming more like religion or religion becoming more like sports on the question of beliefs or any other question, we adhere to the postsecularist view that one can adopt both options simultaneously. Just as one has faith within a religious framework, one can find faith within an athletic framework. Just as belief may fall short of its religious promise, so it may also be for the fan who believes. Just as there is room for belief in both cultural institutions—religion and sports—there is no reason to disregard or exaggerate its expression when it is made public. The postsecularist approach offers a way of accommodating a multitude of beliefs, religious- or sports-related, without establishing a hierarchy where one takes precedence over the other. Whatever the case may be, belief remains a useful means of ameliorating those situations in contemporary life where evidence is absent or not apparent.

2
SACRIFICE

Sacrifice is a term used in a variety of contexts in America. A soldier sacrifices the comfort of being home to fight a war abroad and may have to sacrifice his or her life in the process. Citizens are asked to give up hard-earned money in the form of taxes, some amounts more sacrificial than others, for the good of the country. Fathers and mothers sacrifice time for their children, though this may be a labor of love. Volunteers in all kinds of service sacrifice their time, energy, and money to help those in need. In all of these cases, one must give up something valuable so that a later benefit will come, whether the one sacrificing is the beneficiary or the sacrifice is for another. If nothing valuable or cherished is given up, nothing is truly sacrificed.

The act of sacrifice is as old as religion itself. From the moment that humans held notions about gods or spirits, concerns were raised about how to appease them and earn their favor. At times, in order to gain divine favor, more radical efforts were needed to put a community back in good standing with the spirit world. Bold actions often consisted in the offering of costly spices, a portion of the yearly crop, an animal, or even a fellow human being as a burnt sacrifice. First and foremost, the sacrificed object had to be of value to the community for the gods to respond. Second, the rising smoke from the burning of flesh or grain was believed to reach the "nostrils" of the gods, thereby alerting them to the contrition of the sacrificers. Here, sacrifice is an act of propitiation or an act meant to appease an angry god. Droughts, famine, unexpected death—all could be perceived as events caused by a breach in the divine/human relationship.

A breach, such as the kind caused by disobeying one or more divine commands, may be believed to compel a deity to punish the community for disobedience. Here, sacrifice serves as a ritualistic act designed to make amends and repair the damaged relationship. In addition to mending a breach, a sacrifice can also be an expression of devotion to the divine or to an ultimate truth. From animal sacrifices performed in ancient Hindu rites, to human sacrifice carried out by the ancient Aztecs, to acts of suicidal self-immolation committed by some Buddhists to the belief that Jesus was sacrificed on a cross, we can see that sacrifice is a fundamental concept in religion, despite its varying manifestations.

Sacrifice in the Bible

At the beginning of the Bible, we observe the continuing practice of sacrifice inherited from the pagan world. In the story of Abraham's binding of his son, Isaac, God says:

> "Abraham!" And he said, "Here I am." He (God) said, "Take your son, your only son Isaac, whom you love, and go to the land of Moriah, and offer him there as a burnt-offering on one of the mountains that I shall show you."
>
> (Genesis 22:1–2)

Abraham obeys this call, and when God sees his obedience, God allows him to replace his son with a ram as the object of sacrifice. As alarming as this story may be to modern readers, it must be noted that the act of sacrificing an animal or in extreme circumstances, a child, was commonplace in Abraham's day. And more importantly for later Jewish understandings of the story is that for the first time God places a limit on the kinds of sacrifices that are demanded. God may have severely tested Abraham's faith, but after Abraham passes the test by willingly obeying the command, no longer will God ask for such a drastic act of propitiation.

Rules are later laid out in Jewish Law for the practice of sacrifice. In addition to times, places (the Temple primarily), and who can perform sacrifices, a rationale is also cited:

> For the life of the flesh is in the blood; and I have given it to you for making atonement for your souls on the altar; for, as life, it is the blood that makes atonement . . . For the life of every creature—its blood is its life . . .
>
> (Leviticus 17:11, 14)

Here, God gives life, and life is represented most accurately by the blood that runs through our veins. Therefore, the offering of blood in a sacrifice is symbolic of the giving up of a life in order to get something as valuable as a life in return. Atonement means reconciliation with God, and therefore, the offering of an animal's blood through sacrifice is believed to have the effect of atoning for the state of human souls, thus reconciling the community once again to God.

The theme of atonement through sacrifice is central to Christianity as well. However complicated and disputed by scholars some of these transitions from early pagan cultures to Jewish laws to later Christian practices are, it should be noted that the general function of sacrifice remains intact throughout biblical history. The early Christian Church believed, more than the Jews, that a deep and possibly permanent split from God occurred when Adam and Eve first disobeyed God in the Garden of Eden, later called the "Original Sin." The sacrificing of animals that followed the letter of the law diligently or any human action, no matter how bold, would be insufficient to make up for this primal act of disobedience.

Hence, later Christians held that only a sacrifice of monumental importance could set things right. It is the self-sacrifice of Jesus Christ, who is believed to be both God and man, that established itself as the sole act that could possibly make things right again. In this version of a grand atonement theory, the father gives up his only son as a sacrificial lamb, just like Abraham did with Isaac. Then, the son, Jesus, willingly (unlike a child or a real lamb) gives up his own life for others on the cross. As it's interpreted in the New Testament:

> [Jesus] did not enter by means of the blood of goats and calves; but he entered the Most Holy Place once for all by his own blood, thus obtaining eternal redemption. The blood of goats and bulls and the ashes of a heifer sprinkled on those who are ceremonially unclean sanctify them so that they are outwardly clean. How much more, then, will the blood of Christ, who through the eternal Spirit offered himself unblemished to God, cleanse our consciences from acts that lead to death, so that we may serve the living God!
>
> (Hebrews 9:12–14)

Likewise, Paul writes in his letter to the Romans:

> [S]ince all have sinned and fall short of the glory of God, they are now justified by his grace as a gift, through the redemption that is in Christ Jesus, whom God put forward as a sacrifice of atonement by his blood, effective through faith.
>
> (Romans 3:23–24)

Here, as in the book of Hebrews, the blood that stands in for life still plays an important role in satisfying God, as it did in ancient times. But the key difference for Christians is that in the case of the sacrifice of Jesus, a human community gave up and continues to give up nothing of its own—the benefits of this sacrifice were given once-and-for-all through the work of Jesus himself. And as is found throughout the New Testament, the belief in the importance of this sacrifice effectively reverses the spell of Adam and Eve's first sin and miraculously and mysteriously accomplishes the forgiveness of all sins for all who believe in it.

With the recasting of sacrifice into the Christian story, along with the complete elimination of sacrificial offerings in Judaism around this same time, sacrifice ceases to be an *external* event that uses outside objects in Jewish and Christian religious communities. It transforms into an *internal* event whereby one placates God by sacrificing one's own interests and desires for the sake of others. Paul sacrificing his own sexual desire by remaining celibate while he awaits the Second Coming stands as a good example. This commitment of Paul's is still apparent in the Catholic Church where nuns, monks, and priests remain celibate but think of themselves as married to the Church—a sacrifice none-theless! Similarly, some Catholic orders renounce material possessions and devote their life to prayer and a life of simplicity (Franciscan or Benedictine orders, for instance). In an extreme case, the monks of the Trappist community often sacrifice the comforts of verbal com-munication as they speak only when necessary.

Some give up the comforts that come with being a part of a community in order to attain a spiritual height. Asceticism, a common practice in both Eastern and Western religions, is a term used to describe a lifestyle that involves such sacrifice. The ascetic suppresses the need to satisfy basic human wants and desires such as social camaraderie and worldly success or in extreme cases, food, by leaving the community for long periods of time. Ascetic practices were lived out by the Buddha, Muhammad, and in the New Testament asceticism are seen in the figures of John the Baptist, Jesus, and Paul, to name a few.

Another, more extreme act of sacrifice in certain religious traditions is martyrdom. A martyr, in a very general sense, is ostracized or even killed by others for daring to believe in some truth in the face of great opposition to that truth and/or to those who hold it. The martyr's giving up of a life is the ultimate sacrifice in the name of religion. For example, self-immolation, or the suicidal setting oneself on fire, practiced by some Buddhists and Hindus represents a spiritual yet also provocative act meant to draw attention to the truth that they believe in while also dying for it. It is believed to be an act of reverence to the divine or to an ultimate reality that calls for such acts. Additionally, early Christian martyrs willingly turned themselves into the Roman government for execution because they believed that following Jesus' similar path was the only way to live out the Gospel, as they comprehended it.

Sacrifice in Sports

The idea of sacrifice has carried over from religion into all areas of life, including the sports world. While the details of the act of sacrifice have undergone alterations through history, the underlying logic of it—that giving up something of value results in gaining something else of value—has not changed. For the athlete, there are two primary forms of sacrifice: that which is done for personal gain and that which benefits a group, such as a team or even a nation. Generally speaking, sacrifice is necessary in sports because very little is *given* to an athlete without something being given up in return. While it is true that some are born with superior talent or grow up in a nurturing environment, hard work is always required to cultivate talent or to take advantage of one's surroundings. Every athlete at the highest level has talent. What distinguishes the best from the second-best is often the amount of extra work put in.

On the individual level, if winning is the payoff for sacrifice in sports, what exactly is given up? For those who get up early in the morning to work out, sleep is sacrificed. Since childhood Michael Phelps, who won eight gold medals in the 2008 Olympics in swimming, woke up every day at five o'clock in the morning to train in the pool. Hershel Walker, ex-football star, has done 3,500 sit-ups and 1,000 push-ups every morning since high school. Tiger Woods is on the driving range hitting golf balls most mornings for two hours before playing a practice round at noon. Sleep is certainly sacrificed in these cases.

For those who adhere to a strict, healthy diet, the freedom to eat whatever you want whenever you want is sacrificed. Usain Bolt, who holds world records in the 100- and 200-meter dash, sticks to a highly regimented diet that abides by the ratio of 60 percent protein, 30 percent carbohydrates, and 10 percent fats. Wrestlers have to meet a weight requirement to qualify for a certain weight class, which means that they either have to put on a lot of weight in a short amount of time or lose pounds quickly in time for the next weigh-in before a competition. The independence to eat what one wants, when one wants is sacrificed.

For teenagers who travel weekly for track meets, a normal social life is sacrificed. For instance, Henry Cejudo, 2008 Olympic gold-medal winner in wrestling, said that he had to give up his family, friends, going to the prom, and participating in his high school graduation because of his training regimen. Girls who want to compete in the Olympics in gymnastics usually spend all of their time growing up away from their family and friends at professionally run gyms. The security and comfort of home is sacrificed.

The payoff, of course, is the satisfaction of performing at the highest national or international level, and perhaps ending up being the best at your sport. Michelle Kwan, Olympic skater, says:

> It's tough, but in the back of my mind I realize there are certain things that you have to give up in order to achieve something. My goals are so great and I feel it's worth that sacrifice. Sometimes my body is aching, but I always think, "Why am I in this? Why do I love it so much?" That's what makes me persevere, that's what makes me keep on going.

It is the nature of the goal, a gold medal in the Olympics in Kwan's case, that is so valuable, the sacrifice is worth it in the end. Those who are not willing to put in the time to excel will never be ultimately successful. This is why individual sacrifice is a crucial component of sports.

Yet what may seem a sacrifice to some may be simply delayed gratification for others. In a culture accustomed to immediate gratification, long hours of training spent for the promise that you *might* do better in the future is not simply a physical sacrifice but also a psychological hardship that may, in the end, be left with an unfilled promise. What if I hurt myself training? What if I never make the team no matter how hard I work? What if the coach has an axe to grind against me for something that has nothing to do with performance? And in cases where I am still too young to drive myself, the strain placed on family and friends to shuttle me back and forth from home to the next sporting event can be experienced as a sacrifice for those involved with the athlete's success. This kind of sacrifice, that which brings in the concerns of one's close community, may bring a kind of delayed gratification but any suspension of immediate gratification, in today's society can rightly be viewed as a sacrifice.

While one can conceive of a sacrifice in an individual sport, such as golf, that benefits the player alone, in team sports, sacrifice is necessarily performed for the benefit of others. Not every player can be the superstar—each must give up minutes of playing time for others to play as well as be okay with only one or two players shining at the end. Only one gets to take the final shot or be the last leg in a relay race. Setting a pick or screen in basketball, checking an opponent in hockey or blocking in the sport of cycling (the practice of legally impeding opposing riders to allow a teammate to keep a lead) serve as examples in sports that usually do not get much attention but act to help other teammates succeed. Hence, most of the other members of any team must sacrifice their own need for accolades for the sake of the team's success. This "team-based" type of sacrifice involves less deprivation of creature comforts than many other types of sacrifices in sports because it is more of a denial of one's own glory, not sleep, for the sake of the team. For example, star athletes have been known to take less money so that the team's owner can pay more to other players. Professional basketball player, Kevin Garnett, signed a contract to play for less than he was worth so that his team in 2003, the Minnesota Timberwolves, could sign other players. At the time, Garnett said:

> I didn't need to break the bank. Just because you have some leverage, you know? My thing, man, I want to be on a solid team and I like it here. I wanted to show Mac (general manager Kevin McHale) and the organization it's not always about dough.

Similarly, when players remain loyal to a team in a city that may not be as glamorous as other locations, it is often viewed as a sacrificial act. They are seen to be sacrificing a life on the big stage of New York or Los Angeles to live in a smaller market, such as Green Bay, Wisconsin, or Oklahoma City. When LeBron James decided to leave the Cleveland Cavaliers (near his hometown of Akron, Ohio) for the glitzy Miami Heat in the summer of 2010, he took less money but was still viewed as a traitor by many in Cleveland. Staying in Cleveland would have been seen as a sacrifice, both for the teammates he left behind as well as for the Cavaliers' fans.

Alternatively, when a player refuses to sacrifice his or her own exorbitant earning potential to help the team, even when the sacrifice is not a lot of money relatively speaking, criticism follows. Fans of the Los Angeles Lakers were upset when their star center, Shaquille O'Neal, turned down the opportunity to take a little less money when the team could benefit from the small shortfall in his pocketbook in 2004. A defiant O'Neal reacted, "I won't be devalued. Never, ever devalued. I will never take less than what I am worth. I'm the one that's bringing the players in anyway. And I can bring in players for no money." Paying him *fair* value will end up helping the team, so O'Neal says. But fans read between the lines here—he wanted to save face by talking about his concern for the team while declining to give up anything of real worth to him.

The term sacrifice even makes its way into the terminology of sports from time to time. There are situations in baseball when a player is asked to lay down a bunt or hit a deep fly ball—both plays are almost guaranteed outs for the hitter (though not damaging to his or her statistics)—in order to advance a runner on the bases. It is called a "sacrifice bunt" or "sacrifice fly" because the player gives up the chance to get a hit so that the team can move closer to victory. A story serves to illustrate another kind of sacrifice in baseball. In 1941, Ted Williams was hitting .39955 in batting average (which would have been rounded up to .400 in the final tally) with two games to go in the season. No one had hit .400 in 16 years, nor has anyone in the last 70 years. Williams was given the option to sit out the last two games to protect his batting average. He refused to do so, thus putting his team ahead of an individual record. He happened to go 6 for 8 at the plate in the last two games, raising his final average to .406. When asked about his decision to play, he responded coyly that he didn't really deserve the .400 average if he sat out. It was not only a sacrifice for the team, but one for the integrity of the game on the whole for Williams.

Sacrifice and Religion Today

The value of sacrifice in religion has been retained even after the slaughter and burning of external objects ceased to be a common practice in Judaism and Christianity over 2,000 years ago. Recall that this historical development saw the move of sacrifice from the external to the internal. One's own desire, goals, and ego (all thought to stand in the way of God's will) needed to be brought to the "altar" for destruction. However, the internalization of sacrifice has resulted in some unintended consequences that can be observed today. While the notion that one must give up valuable parts of oneself for God is still preached, the act of giving up something valuable for a larger cause has largely vanished from the lives of many religious Americans, especially Christians. It is not that the belief that sacrifice is central to one's Christian faith has gone away—Christ's death on the cross is heard in sermons preached each Sunday to this day. Nor has the belief that one must be "crucified with Christ" (Galatians 2:20) in order to be saved disappeared from the minds of adherents. Yet if sacrifice only exists as a compelling idea but is not something to be practiced in one's daily life, why aren't Christians currently practicing what their pastors preach and their Bible dictates?

One of the primary cultural developments of the twentieth century in America that has changed the way Americans think about themselves is the rise of consumer culture. Americans are now taught to think and act like consumers or shoppers for everything from entertainment, careers, education, and churches, all the way to how and where they worship God. This kind of mindset generates a "customer is always right" mentality and demands a response from the seller of these "commodities" in order to step up and keep customers happy. When the satisfaction of desire is the goal of a purchase and the seller of a product must make sure that consumer desire is satisfied in the religious arena, the way God is thought of is affected mightily. In a consumer culture, religious shoppers (or seekers as they are often called) may desire a church that does not focus on uncomfortable concepts, such as sin, judgment or Hell, and a God that does not demand difficult or undesirable actions, such as sacrifice. And in response, many churches will deliver messages stripped of concepts with sharp edges so that customers keep returning. Sacrifice, as one might imagine, is one of those concepts with particularly sharp edges.

The German theologian, Dietrich Bonhoeffer (1906–1945), captures this new reality well when he discusses the Christian concept of grace. Grace is God's gift of salvation granted to sinners even though it is not deserved, but simply given. Bonhoeffer, though, claims:

> Cheap grace is the grace we bestow on ourselves. Cheap grace is the preaching of forgiveness without requiring repentance, baptism without church discipline, Communion without

confession . . . Cheap grace is grace without discipleship, grace without the cross, grace without Jesus Christ, living and incarnate.

(Bonhoeffer 1995, 44)

One could add to his list, "getting what you want without sacrifice." Alternatively, for Bonhoeffer:

[Costly grace] calls us to follow Jesus Christ. It is costly because it costs a man his life, and it is grace because it gives a man the only true life . . . Above all, it is costly because it cost God the life of his Son: "ye were bought at a price," and what has cost God much cannot be cheap for us.

(Ibid., 45)

Bonhoeffer contrasts these two types of grace because he is disturbed by the number of Christians in the early twentieth century who only want grace without the high cost. Instead, it is the very idea of sacrifice that is threaded through his description of costly grace. According to this view, the sacrifice of Jesus is costly to himself and to God while Christians receive the benefits of salvation in the form of grace. Therefore, to receive grace and its benefits, one must be willing to spend or sacrifice costly things in a corresponding way. It could be argued that cheap grace fits comfortably into a consumer culture in that it satisfies the desire to gain a *version* of grace, but costly grace requires the kind of sacrifice that will not sit well within the consumer mindset.

Against Bonhoeffer's wishes, many Christian churches now promote theologies that meet the religious consumers or seekers where they are, which is entrenched in a consumer culture. For example, a "Gospel of Prosperity" boldly asserts that God wants everyone to be rich, both materially and psychologically (though some churches emphasize one over the other). Indeed, a full 61 percent of American Christians believe that God wants them to be prosperous, which helps explain the popularity of such a movement. Despite Jesus' words to the contrary, "it is easier for a camel to go through the eye of a needle than for someone who is rich to enter the kingdom of God" (Matthew

19:24), some Gospel of Prosperity preachers claim that material wealth is a sign from God that one is blessed. Praying for money, visualizing money entering a bank account, maintaining overall positive thoughts: all are techniques for getting rich, and thus are ways to please God in the process.

Less crass are the pastors who contend that God wants you to be happy or psychologically prosperous. Again, emotional contentment is viewed as a blessing from God. And likewise, petitioning God for happiness or positive thoughts is the most common path to align oneself to God's will. Joel Osteen, pastor of the largest church in America located in Houston, Texas, mixes financial and emotional prosperity in the following quote:

> Does God want us to be rich? When I hear that word rich, I think people say, "Well, he's preaching that everybody's going to be a millionaire." I don't think that's it. I preach that anybody can improve their lives. I think God wants us to be prosperous. I think he wants us to be happy. To me, you need to have money to pay your bills. I think God wants us to send our kids to college. I think he wants us to be a blessing to other people. But I don't think I'd say God wants us to be rich. It's all relative, isn't it?
>
> (Van Beima and Chu 2006)

If "God wants us to be happy," then concepts such as Hell, divine judgment, or mortal sin can be seen as obstacles to living out God's will. Likewise, to no surprise, the word "sacrifice" is underplayed in the language of the Gospel of Prosperity.

There are other churches or ministries in the United States that do demand sacrifice, yet endorse a certain way of thinking about it—that which caters to the interests of men. Organizations such as Promise Keepers and the Fellowship of Christian Athletes center on male strength as a fundamental aspect of the male (and female!) Christian journey. They readily use sports as a metaphor to speak of the ways in which men can achieve their ideal position in marriage and as fathers. Promise Keepers' founder and former University of Colorado head football coach, Bill McCartney, said that its mission is to "celebrate Biblical manhood and motivate men toward a Christ-like masculinity."

Sacrifice is a constant theme in these organizations as men must suppress their so-called natural instincts for domination in order to attain the kind of relationships of which Jesus would approve.

And sports supplies a perfect vehicle for carrying men to this goal. If one can equate the suppression of instincts (read sacrifice) needed to excel at sports to life, then one can certainly understand the sacrifice necessary to be a good husband and father. Despite the popularity of such movements, the question still remains: If sports plus man-talk is needed to transmit the message of sacrifice, does it bear any relation to the original intent of Biblical sacrifices? Perhaps, but clearly the message of sacrifice as promoted by Promise Keepers must run through a gauntlet of appealing cultural channels that may or may not have any connection to the Bible: what man wouldn't want to be a biblical hero and use athleticism to get there?

The practice of costly sacrifice, as conveyed in the Bible, has performed a kind of disappearing act when it comes to contemporary churches wishing to stay relevant. Even though sacrifice has historically been tightly interwoven with religious belief and practice since its beginnings and the term is still uttered with reverence from the pulpit, the act of giving up something costly does not play well in a consumer culture where benefits are expected in return for little or no real cost. Nor does it fit into a theology that proclaims that God prefers humanity to have an easy, happy, and wealthy life as opposed to one filled with struggle, pain, and sacrifice. Not that these latter three have departed from everyday life—they have merely been downplayed in or even eliminated from much religious discourse in America.

Sacrifice in Religion and Sports

Since Americans seem to have a greater fluency when discussing sports, entertainment, and politics rather than deep issues in theology, it is not surprising that we find long-standing religious concepts, such as sacrifice, present in these secular contexts. The legacy that religion has left us with and its articulation of the role and expectations of sacrifice lends itself well to these discourses. But the fact that Americans are more comfortable thinking about sacrifice in the context of sports rather than in a religious context is somewhat perplexing, given the central role sacrifice plays in the Biblical narratives. Maybe religious institutions, as we argued above, are more concerned with coddling their congregants than speaking hard truths. And perhaps athletes are more wired to take a hit for the team than parishioners are for God. Athletes may be more aware that greatness requires sacrifice than church-goers who believe that it is already a great sacrifice simply to attend church each Sunday morning. Or given the power of the idea of internal sacrifice, parishioners may be thinking that sacrifice is a personal exercise that they can accomplish on their own rather than that which serves a community of worshippers to whom they are accountable. Churches are then tempted to minimize the burdens of discipleship so that potential members are not scared away for good.

But it is exactly the test of faith that sacrifice was supposed to address, whether in the case of Abraham and Isaac or Jesus' death on the cross. In both the cases of Abraham and of Jesus, sacrifice was a matter of life and death. As we have seen in the previous section, that kind of sacrifice is not expected in most American religious lives anymore; it is relegated to the medical (organ donation, for example) and military arenas. Yet the language and the conceptual underpinnings of sacrifice remain powerful in pursuits that are not life-threatening. One such arena, as we saw in the second section, is sports. This is why we should not be confused or offended when we find sacrifice language in sports. If Kellen Winslow Jr., a tight end for the Miami Hurricanes in 2003, was confused about whether he was an athlete or a soldier while playing football after claiming that football was war, the public cleared it up for him quickly and he responded in kind. In his apology for equating sports to war, he said:

> As for my reference to being a soldier in a war, I meant no disrespect to the men and women who have served, or are currently serving, in the armed forces. I cannot begin to imagine the magnitude of war or its consequences.

Sacrifice language in the sports world, because it does not truly depict life-or-death scenarios, more closely functions like the language that flows from the contemporary American pulpit on Sundays. Both discourses utilize the *gravity* of the idea of sacrifice without the dire consequences that can result when the sacrifice of one's life is involved. Both have the luxury of drawing on stories in which people did sacrifice their lives to convey a truth about both respective sets of activities without having to act those stories out literally. In other words, contemporary American religion and sports need the concept of sacrifice to convey meaning but stop short of asking for the ultimate sacrifice. Hence, both religion and sports use the concept of sacrifice similarly on the level of cultural communication, despite what one may think of this "softer" use of the term.

This makes sense when looked at through the lens of postsecularism. Because sports figures or religious leaders are using the idea of sacrifice in similar but different ways, they thereby reinforce in each other a commitment to a life of sacrifice on behalf of a community (team or church) as well as a deeply held belief (victory or salvation). There are those who suggest that our obsession with sports has become our American religion, a replacement of sorts. And it should be admitted that, given the cultural prominence of sports, it is reasonable that religious forms of sacrifice will be expressed by the athletes that fans follow. But what is forgotten in this scenario is the realization that the very language of sacrifice and the different forms it has taken in history remains unshaken. If some religious institutions refrain from demanding personal sacrifice of their congregations, it's unfortunate but not tragic. The lessons have not been completely forgotten. What else could motivate an athlete to train every morning since childhood to chase a piece of gold worn around the neck? While the pursuit of Olympic gold may be able to justify itself in today's culture, there must be a remnant of that old-time religious fervor to please a permanent, transcendent ideal that underlies the daily sacrifices of the athlete. Otherwise, anyone's spirit would be broken quickly if the goal was truly conceived as merely material and hence, fleeting.

It is in this sense that as much as religion informs sports in language and ideas, so does American sports teach our culture the lessons of personal sacrifice on behalf of a team or community. Looking at both of these important cultural institutions as educational sources rather than as entertainment or generators of catch phrases holds the possibility of enhancing a sense of community and reinvigorating the value of personal sacrifice.

If there is any postsecularist insight that emerges from our examination of sacrifice it is that, while more apparent in the lives of political leaders, such as Gandhi and Martin Luther King, Jr., sacrifice can also be observed frequently in the lives of athletes. Though only rarely associated with murder or death threats, sports provides a constant reminder of the pervasiveness of sacrifice among athletes, their families, and their fans. By drawing on religious antecedents, its actual practices make sports as relevant a cultural drama as anything found in religious or political institutions today.

3
RELICS

It is common for people to give more value to certain material objects over others. A wedding ring handed down through generations will be of more worth than a ring bought at a store. A home previously owned by a celebrity will fetch more on the market than a similar house whose owners are not famous. A piece of the Berlin Wall holds much more significance and value than a rock of similar composition found in nature. Even though the material properties of each of these pairs of items do not differ greatly to the senses, we tend to endow some objects with added meaning despite their similarity to "less fortunate" objects. We add sentimental value to objects passed down from special people in our lives, cultural value to objects touched by famous people, and historical value to objects that were part of momentous occasions.

A relic is a material item that can be endowed with *religious* significance. The word comes from the Latin, *reliquiae*, meaning "remains" or "something left behind." As such, important religious leaders have left fingernails, hair, and bones behind when they die. In many religions, these bodily relics are enshrined in sacred places and venerated by followers. In addition, some religious leaders' clothing, jewelry, tombstones, and even the land that they walked on or the water they swam in can also act as relics that have been left behind or "relinquished."

The use of material objects to inform religious beliefs and practices has a long history. Pre-biblical religions observed a practice called *totemism* whereby material objects were believed to possess sacred value that connected the religious community to the divine. Totems included minerals, plants, jewelry, animals, and even human beings in some cases. Often, totems embodied some of the fundamental myths that informed the community of their origins and enabled a community to gain solidarity around the totem or a representation of it. The Native American Cherokee tribe, for instance, made the turtle its totem because the members believed that the world was formed on a turtle's back. It was prohibited or taboo to eat turtles. And places where images of turtles were painted, sometimes on a "totem pole," were holy sites that would bind the tribe to the totem and protect it. The totem did not simply *represent* the spirit world; it *housed* actual spirits in its material casing, too. Though totems were not worshipped in the modern sense of the word, they served as material representations of the non-material world, thus allowing a relationship with spirits through a material substance.

While this practice of revering special material objects is rejected by some religions, the existence of religious relics in almost every religion should make sense to us. Many tend to hang on to material objects when abstract ideas of the divine can be fleeting and doubted as to their truth. There has always been a reliance on the sense of touch and sight to understand the world, and therefore people naturally need durable objects to ground their faith and help them connect with the non-material spiritual realm from time to time.

Relics in the Bible

With the onset of monotheism (worship of one God), a different, more complex relationship between material objects and the spiritual realm develops. Because of the common use of statues and amulets in polytheism (worship of multiple gods), the shift to the belief in one God eventually resulted in a deep skepticism that anything material could compete with that one God. The first of the Ten Commandments reflects this concern: "You shall have no other gods before me," and is followed by the more specific second commandment:

> You shall not make for yourself an idol, whether in the form of anything that is in heaven above, or that is on the earth beneath, or that is in the water under the earth. You shall not bow down to them or worship them; for I the Lord your God am a jealous God.
>
> (Exodus 20:3–5)

These commandments prohibit idolatry or the worshiping of anything besides God, and they stand as the first, and hence, the primary instructions for the Israelites to follow.

However, while the Israelites were waiting for Moses to come down from Mount Sinai to deliver the commandments, in their impatience they reverted back to their old ways. A golden calf was crafted from melted jewelry, danced around, worshipped, and offered sacrifices. This is a clear violation of a divine command, as is revealed in God's instructions to Moses after seeing what the Israelites had done:

> Go down, because your people, whom you brought up out of Egypt, have become corrupt. They have been quick to turn away from what I commanded them and have made themselves an idol cast in the shape of a calf. They have bowed down to it and sacrificed to it and have said, "These are your gods, Israel, who brought you up out of Egypt."
>
> (Exodus 32:7–8)

As is conveyed here, it is not anything human-made that has the power to bring the Israelites out of slavery in Egypt, but the one God, with whom no material object can compete. This passage also demonstrates that the veneration and even worship of that which can be touched and seen is a real temptation when an invisible, intangible God understandably seems distant from the natural world.

In Christianity there is a similar hierarchy upheld between the spiritual and material, with the former holding a superior position, though the way that the material relates to the spiritual is different from Jewish understandings. The Gospels present Jesus as one who is more concerned with the *attitude* held toward the material world rather than the power that can be given to particular material objects. When asked by some people hostile to Jesus' message about the lawfulness of paying taxes, as cited before, Jesus says:

> "Show me the coin used for paying the tax." They brought him a denarius, and he asked them, "Whose portrait is this? And whose inscription?" "Caesar's," they replied. Then he said to them, "Give to Caesar what is Caesar's, and to God what is God's."
>
> (Matthew 22:19–21)

The coin is used by Jesus as a material representation of Caesar, not as an idol. He does not suggest that the coins are being worshipped as an idol, or prohibit or criticize the use of the coin to pay taxes. Instead, the coin is a material instrument acting to illustrate the radical difference between worldly commerce and religious devotion, thereby making clear that one's attitude toward the things of God should also be different from the attitude toward material things.

As found in the Gospel of John, Jesus again does not denigrate the material completely in the face of the spiritual but upholds both as necessary while managing to honor the spirit more than the material flesh.

> I tell you the truth, no one can enter the kingdom of God unless he is born of water and the Spirit. Flesh gives birth to flesh, but the Spirit gives birth to spirit. You should not be surprised at my saying, "You must be born again." The wind blows wherever it pleases. You hear its sound, but you cannot tell where it comes from or where it is going. So it is with everyone born of the Spirit.
>
> (John 3: 5–8)

All are born of water (flesh) and spirit, so both are necessary. Yet it is a spiritual birth that Jesus is emphasizing because he is talking about being "born again." Obviously one cannot have a second physical birth, so it is a rebirth in the spirit that offers the ability to be born again.

Paul accepts this separation between the material and spiritual but puts one above the other more boldly than Jesus seems to. One can interpret his discussion of the dichotomy between the spirit and the flesh as saying that the material flesh is that which tempts one into sexual perversion, gluttony, and pride, while the spiritual part of us represses the fleshly desires with the help of the power of God. In his letter to the Galatians, Paul writes:

> Live by the Spirit, I say, and do not gratify the desires of the flesh . . . the works of the flesh are obvious: fornication, impurity, licentiousness . . . By contrast, the fruit of the Spirit is love, joy, peace, patience, kindness, generosity, faithfulness, gentleness, and self-control.

> (Galatians 5:16, 19, 22–23)

While the flesh, as Paul perceives it, is not an idol that can be worshipped per se, it is the material, embodied part of us that leads to the destructive drive to satisfy material wants. In particular, Paul highlights sexual immorality as a set of behaviors that draw out the distinction between the material and the spiritual most profoundly.

> Do you not know that he who unites himself with a prostitute is one with her in body? For it is said, "The two will become one flesh." But he who unites himself with the Lord is one with him in spirit. Flee from sexual immorality. All other sins a man commits are outside his body, but he who sins sexually sins against his own body. Do you not know that your body is a temple of the Holy Spirit, who is in you, whom you have received from God? You are not your own; you were bought at a price. Therefore honor God with your body.

> (1 Corinthians 6:16–20)

The flesh tempts, but it is also an unavoidable fact of human existence. The proper way to think of our bodies, according to Paul, is to consider them properties of God, not our own. And the stamp on our fleshly bodies that identifies them as God's property is not a material mark but the presence of the Holy Spirit. The body is merely a temple, important to maintain and not defile, but it is the spirit within the material temple that makes it so.

Jewish proscriptions against idolatry combined with Paul's warning about the temptations of the flesh leave a legacy of a certain kind of relationship between material objects and the faithful. This, however, does not mean that the relationship has been lived out in the same way for the last 2,000 years. The Catholic Church as well as the Orthodox Church have historically stressed the value of icons (material representations) to convey Biblical truths. Stained glass windows depicting the apostles and later saints, crosses with the deceased Jesus hanging on them, statues of the Virgin Mary, and even the elaborate churches themselves, are all iconic presentations. These icons are material in nature, but religious relics do not have to be considered iconic or that which carries a religious truth. More typical religious relics can vary from the mundane, such as the rosary, a string of beads meant to guide prayers to Mary, to the extraordinary. For an example of the latter, take the Sudarium of Oviedo, which is believed to be the bloodstained cloth used to wrap Jesus' head after the crucifixion and which is held in a church in Spain. Most notable is the Shroud of Turin, the piece of cloth believed to have been placed on the body of Jesus at the time of his burial. For believers, the power of the shroud does not rest only in its historical significance; it displays an image of a face (the face of Jesus?) that adds another level of authenticity to this special material relic.

Part of the justification for the use of icons and relics in some Christian churches has to do with the incarnation of Jesus Christ. If an immaterial God became material flesh in the person of Jesus, Jewish prohibitions against carved images can be reinterpreted and even softened as a license, of sorts, can be given to the materialization of holy figures and events. If God can become flesh, then God may inhabit other material items too. The doctrine of transubstantiation in the Catholic Church is a theological expression of this position. It states that during a properly performed communion, the bread and wine transform into the actual body and blood of Christ. Similarly, Mormons believe that their prophet, Joseph Smith, encountered the *bodily* form of God and Jesus in a grove of trees as the first of his many visions. Even though it is believed by most Christians that God became flesh in the form of Jesus Christ, material substances are *never* to be worshipped as such. They are to be venerated or respected as physical signs that point beyond themselves to God.

This last warning from Christian thinkers about the danger of material objects becoming more than what they really are has not stopped critics of the practice of iconophilia (the love of icons) from having their say. Perhaps Muhammad's most significant act was to destroy the various statues of Arabian gods that surrounded and filled the inside of the *Ka'ba* in Mecca, the holiest site for Muslims. Full submission to God (Allah) means not only eliminating material competitors for God's devotion but never even drawing a picture of God or of the prophet Muhammad. In full alignment with the first two commandments, Muhammad forcefully rejects idolatry in this way. As Islamic reasoning goes, such representations could tempt observers to submit to the image, as if it contained divine power, thus drawing attention away from the only entity worthy of full submission: God.

Similarly, one of the defining characteristics of the Protestant Reformation, begun by Martin Luther in 1517, is its reaction to the Catholic Church's use of material icons and relics. Some Reformers were in full support of iconoclasm, or the destruction of icons. Much of this reaction stemmed from Luther's notion of *sola scriptura*: reading the Bible alone is sufficient to learn God's truth. This idea served to render unnecessary the physical presence of the Church and its priests as intermediaries that purportedly helped put congregants into relationship with God. French Reformed theologian, John Calvin (1509–1564), writes in his magnum opus, *Institutes of the Christian Religion*, that the use of religious icons always goes far beyond mere admiration or veneration.

> When men thought they gazed upon God in images, they also worshiped him in them. Finally, all men, having fixed their minds and eyes upon them, began to grow more brutish and to be overwhelmed with admiration for them, as if something of divinity inhered there . . . Therefore, when you prostrate yourself in veneration, representing to yourself in an image either a god or a creature, you are already ensnared in some superstition.
>
> (1960, 109)

The veneration of icons, because of our sinful, weak nature, can quickly become worship, even though it is really superstition. Icons, which

Catholics use as a *means* for worshipping God, may turn into an end in themselves. Hence, like Muhammad, Calvin was particularly wary of the mere presence of icons and relics in the places of worship and homes of the devoted.

The effects of the Reformation can clearly be seen today in the United States. The divine status of consecrated bread and wine under transubstantiation has been replaced by the *symbolic* role of bread and wine in the Protestant ritual of communion. Jesus has been taken off of crosses displayed in most Protestant churches for the same reason—too much focus on the material body of Jesus downplays the belief that it is the resurrection that matters more than the crucifixion. Similarly, the Virgin Mary has been eliminated as a stand-alone figure in most Protestant churches (both in statue form and in sermons) because, unlike her son, she is not believed to be essentially different from all other women. And finally, in some Protestant denominations, the color in stained glass has been removed so that the distraction it creates from true worship is removed.

Relics in Sports

Conversely, material objects are essential in sports. Wooden bats are needed to hit leather-covered baseballs. Sharpened metal blades are needed to skate on ice. Shoulder pads are needed to protect football players from injury. And balls of various sizes and shapes are the centerpiece of most of the sports we enjoy. Without these and other material objects, these sports don't exist. They mediate the sport itself. One may have all the talent in the world and desire the highest levels of success, but to actualize talent and translate it into success, a ball must be kicked, a javelin must be thrown, and a puck must be hit with a stick.

Some objects in sports rise to the level of relics. But because material instruments are part and parcel of sports, there is less of a stigma attached to sports relics than to those found in religion. And because a football jersey stands little chance in a competition with God, placing excess significance on a sports item could not properly be called idolatry. That said, it is true that baseball bats and uniforms used in the Major Leagues hold more significance than similar bats and jerseys bought at the stadium. Even more so, a bat used to hit a historic home run and a jersey worn in important games are often endowed with religious-like significance. How does an inert piece of wood or leather come to be enshrined in a museum, placed on the mantle of a fan's home, or bought for hundreds of thousands of dollars? Or what is the definition of a relic in sports?

As was the case with the concept of belief, whether you are inside or outside the lines on the field makes a big difference in the way that certain material objects are appropriated. For players, not fans, the use of material equipment is, for the most part, strictly functional. Tennis players may distinguish between this or that tennis racket based on its feel and performance but that distinction is made largely on its utility. For elite athletes, money is not an issue (much of their equipment is given to them by companies looking for free advertising), and the look of a piece of equipment is far less important than its ability to get the job done. That said, sports history is filled with stories of athletes endowing what they wear or a piece of their equipment with extra value that transcends their function alone.

This kind of endowment ranges from the subtle to the overtly superstitious. Jason Giambi personally weighs each bat given to him, even though the bat company guarantees consistency, just to make sure they are the same. If Giambi's playing bat is secretly replaced with one of these other bats, he'd probably never know. This is a case in which the functionality of the bat is still the primary concern but Giambi still needs his own added reassurance that the factory cannot supply.

A baseball player who does not want to switch out a bat that he has been using until it breaks is an example of the less subtle expression. On May 8, 2012, Texas Rangers' slugger, Josh Hamilton, became the sixteenth player in baseball history to hit four home runs in a single game. Two pertinent anecdotes emerged from this event. One, Hamilton refused to replace the bat that he used to hit the home runs with until it broke eight days later—a much longer time period than he normally takes to replace any old bat. And two, two of the four home run balls were returned to him by a fellow teammate, and Hamilton was subsequently asked what he was going to do with them. He said, "Uh, I don't know, probably put them in a closet somewhere—they'll probably be thrown around in my backyard by my kids." Hamilton is a dedicated Evangelical Christian, which could explain his resistance to valorizing any material object (recall Calvin), even though he seemed to hang on to his bat for longer than he should have!

Moving into more explicitly superstitious territory, recall that Wade Boggs ate chicken before each game, admitting that the chicken helped him perform better than presumably eating other types of meat with similar nutritional value. And somewhat like Michael Jordan, basketball's Jason Terry sleeps with the uniform shorts of the opposing team the night before a game. Even if a reasonable explanation is given for the use of a material object in sports, that use can still reveal the object's exaggerated value. Athletes such as football's Drew Brees, golf's Hunter Mahan, and baseball's Matt Kemp wear Power Balance bracelets—wristbands that, through a hologram imprinted into the bracelet, are believed to "resonate with and respond to the natural energy field of the body" (Roenigk 2010). Despite the fact that double-blind studies have shown these bracelets to have no effect on performance, they are in part worn because the material in the bracelet is believed to be accomplishing something—a kind of placebo effect may be in operation.

On a related note, during the 2011 baseball playoffs, a squirrel ran onto the field in St. Louis as the Cardinals were playing the Philadelphia Phillies. As St. Louis won that game and progressed through the playoffs towards a championship, the "rally squirrel" was transformed into a good luck charm for the Cardinals' players and fans. Like a modern totemistic animal, the squirrel was seen on T-shirts worn to the games and was even engraved on all of the players' World Series rings. Athletes, as should be expected, minimize the possibility that a piece of equipment or a special meal or a rodent can have special, magical powers. Just as athletes claim not to rely on magical thinking to amplify their performance, they also refuse to lend credence to special bats, hats, or shoes—at least publicly.

Fans, on the other hand, more unabashedly engage and honor the material world of sports. Because they are spectators to the action on the field, most often through a television screen, there exists a significant gap between the player and the fan. Yes, fans know statistics, attend games, and defend their team vociferously in online chat rooms and at social gatherings. While these activities certainly do foster connections between the fans and their team, athletes are on the television screen, and the only recourse left for fans is to cheer on their team or players to fellow fans who are in a similar predicament.

Relics that have ties to players and teams can offer a more tangible bridge between fans and their sport. This bridge-building frequently begins with the first team pennant or poster of a favorite athlete to adorn a child's bedroom wall. These are like icons that serve as daily, durable reminders of an allegiance to a team and/or player in ways that memories cannot reliably reproduce. In addition, young athletes often participate in little leagues of their own, where their team will often adopt the name of a professional team and don the appropriate uniform. Identification with the professional team is forged, albeit a thin bond, through mimicry. Moreover, catching a foul ball at a baseball game, receiving a sweat band from a player after a basketball game, even pulling up a little grass from a famous field are attempts to procure something material from the game itself that serves to identify with the action on the field and remind one of that moment in time.

A level of identification with an athlete can occur in golf that cannot in other sports. If an amateur golfer shoots a 97 at Augusta National Golf Course, which hosts the Masters tournament and where Tiger Woods has shot a 65, the difference between the amateur and Tiger is one of degree—32 shots. There is more of a qualitative difference between the intramural flag football game and an NFL game; identification with professionals is nearly impossible in this case despite the effort to bridge this gap mentally. With golf, it is the same game played with similar equipment on the exact same material landscape that can more closely link a fan to a professional golfer, even if the scores differ greatly. Whereas in football, even if the pick-up game were played on an actual NFL field, the equipment and physical location are not able to broker a similar relationship.

Sports memorabilia constitute, perhaps, the most profound examples of relics to be found in the sports world. It is big business. Common items include collectables such as ticket stubs of big games and rare baseball cards. There is a different category for items gathered from actual sporting events that include jerseys worn during a game, balls, bats, hockey sticks, and helmets, to name a few. Just as in religion, these are ordinary objects that have touched greatness, which immediately converts them into valuable relics. Add a player's or entire team's autograph to one of these, and a legitimacy and authenticity is conferred—a benefit that the Shroud of Turin cannot enjoy.

A foul ball caught at a big league game differs from a baseball in a plastic case sold at a show because the former has personal meaning while the latter is a commodity. An example helps point out the difference. Roger Maris had held the single-season home run record since 1961 leading into the 1998 baseball season. The 1998 season saw an epic battle between Mark McGwire and Sammy Sosa, both of whom seemed poised to shatter one of the most cherished records in sports. McGwire hit home run number 62 on September 8, 1998, and Tim Forneris, a groundskeeper, picked it up in the stands. He had a choice to either give it back to McGwire or sell it on the market for at least a million dollars. He chose to hand it over to McGwire. McGwire's seventieth homerun that season, his last and the one that set the new record, was caught by Philip Ozersky and promptly sold for over three million dollars to a wealthy collector. Without judging the moral worth of the respective decisions, it is important to note that in both cases, a stitched-up leather sphere was ascribed immense value based on when and how it was hit. The difference between these two choices is the type of value given to them by each person. Forneris was quoted as saying after he gave #62 back to McGwire, "It's not mine to begin with. McGwire just lost it, and I brought it home. I'm just a regular Joe." He assumed that McGwire would value the baseball more than himself and further opined that McGwire never really lost the ball when it ended up in Forneris' hands. The ball held *social* value for Forneris in that giving it up would benefit another. Alternatively, the ball held enormous *financial* value for Ozersky when he claimed ownership of it and then allowed the market to assign its own version of value.

This dynamic relationship between social and financial value of sports items is illustrated equally well with trophies. The value of all trophies surpasses the value of the raw materials and labor that went into creating them. Yet not all trophies are created equal. The Lombardi Trophy in professional football, the Claret Jug awarded to golf's British Open champion, the Heisman Trophy given to the best college football player, a gold medal given to the winner of any Olympic event—all are created each year (or every four years in the case of the Olympics) and are retained by the winning team or player in perpetuity. The Stanley Cup, awarded to the National Hockey League champions, however, is a one-time creation and on loan to the winning team until the next winner is crowned.

The trophies that can be kept permanently are privately owned by the winner. They can sell them if they desire, as O.J. Simpson had to do with his 1973 Heisman Trophy. Or, if it is lost or destroyed, as was the case with the crystal football trophy awarded to the 2012 college football champs, the University of Alabama, it can and almost certainly will be replaced. The Stanley Cup, on the other hand, is not privately owned by the team who won it; it is managed by the league. All players, coaches, and staff that were involved in the championship have their names engraved on the trophy dating back to 1893. When a team wins the Stanley Cup, it is routinely passed to each player to have for a day. The trophy travels constantly to schools, churches, and public events on its yearly tour, usually in the city whose team won the Cup. In a long-standing ritual, many players drink out of it and in so doing each player shares in a ritual performed by his own team members and previous winners of years past. Brought around for the community to enjoy, the Cup is thus communal property for at least a year. And when it is passed to the next community of players and fans the following year, the new fans are able to connect with fans of previous communities.

Material objects in sports are necessary features of any game. We often don't think about the role of a basketball during a game as the athletes are the ones who are showcased, and this is the way it should be. However, sports generates relationships with material products for fans and players alike that transcend the physical and chemical composition of the product. Whether the historical, social, sentimental, or financial value added to these items and relics is excessive or not, it should be clear that sports has the capacity to lift mundane matter out of its inert state and endow it with the kind of meaning that approaches the religious.

Relics and Religion Today

The singling out of certain objects for veneration has been met with skepticism and fervor in religion. The tactile immediacy of objects, such as statues, rosaries, or a marble plaque with the Ten Commandments inscribed on it, is at once reassuring and symbolically powerful. Just as is commonly said, "a picture is worth a thousand words," so is a crucifix that tells the Christian story without speaking a word. An entire worldview of the faithful is bundled into one object that can even be worn on a necklace or on a T-shirt. When wearing a cross, Christians acknowledge who they are, what they believe, and what they want others to know. Questions remain, though: Is the cross merely a symbol that points beyond itself to a non-material reality (God), or has it become an object of adulation in and of itself? When Christians stare at the cross or wear it prominently, is it possible to separate its symbolic power embodied in the matter that makes it up from the thing it symbolizes? And finally, is the persistence of relics in contemporary culture an indication that material objects hold human fascination in a way that cannot be solely explained by religion?

The German philosopher and political economist Karl Marx (1818–1883) applies the endowing of certain material objects with more power than they deserve to the production of objects small and large in a capitalist economy. His analysis is a helpful tool for understanding how the current status of religious relics has been shaped by capitalism. Marx argues that commodities, or products created to be sold exclusively on the market instead of used by their creator, are fetishes. Their "fetish quality" is due to the way that they are produced, distributed, bought, and consumed. Many people contribute to the production of say, a watch, which is produced in a watch factory. A factory worker attaches the hands to the face of the watch, another stitches the band, and yet another screws in the gears. All of these people put their labor into a part of the final product, and hence are related to each other through the production of a single watch. However, because they are not making the watch for themselves but for someone to buy on the market, that watch's exchange value or price is measured by its relationship to the prices of other watches or any commodity on the open market. Hidden in the price is the nature of the labor and materials that went into making each watch.

Hence, the exchange value of any commodity is distanced from the human labor that created it, according to Marx. So, to relate to commodities only on the basis of their price when compared to other commodities or money is to endow them with value (exchange) that transcends their real value (use). When we confront commodities in the marketplace, we inadvertently give them a mystical character or we fetishize them. In Marx's words:

> The mysterious character of the commodity-form consists therefore simply in the fact that the commodity reflects the social characteristics of men's own labour as objective characteristics of the product of the labour themselves as the socio-natural properties of these things.
>
> (Marx, 1976, 164–165)

Though seemingly "mysterious," there is no mystery at all as to why certain commodities appear to be worth more than they ought to be, given how useful or useless they are. Appropriately, Marx draws on an analogy from the world of religion to make his point:

> It is nothing but the definite social relations between men themselves which assumes here, for them, the fantastic form of a relation between things. In order, therefore, to find an analogy we must take flight into the misty realm of religion. There the products of the human brain appear as autonomous figures endowed with a life of their own, which enter into relations both with each other and with the human race. So it is in the world of commodities with the products of men's hands.
>
> (Ibid., 165)

Regardless of Marx's critical stance on religion in general (religion is the "opiate of the masses"), in this passage he gestures towards the ability of humans to use their religious ways of thinking to endow meaning to objects that don't deserve such endowment. He wants to make sure that we understand how commodities are produced, who produces them, and what personal hardships—even in the age of machines—people endure to produce them—religion helps him make the point. Commodities have both a use-value—we can use them to feed us, carry us around town, etc.—and an exchange-value—we can trade them with each other or pay the price listed on the item. Yet as we have seen, there is an additional way in which we value certain objects: we admire, revere, or worship them. The cross worn and Josh Hamilton's bat have fetish value as commodities *plus* added value as relics.

Stated another way, commodities in America's hyper-capitalist consumer culture, even religious relics, cannot escape the forces of the marketplace. The religious significance is thereby compromised a bit—do you honor your faith by wearing a hand-made wooden cross on a necklace as much as you do wearing a tasteful gold chain with a cross bought at a store? Alternatively, would it say anything about your commitment to God that you are or are not willing to sacrifice a few dollars for accessories that promote your faith? The switch from the appreciation of the religious value of the relic itself to its use as a fashion statement is subtle but real; there are social pressures and expectations to live up to cultural norms, as given by communities. As members of a consumer society, our interactions with others and ourselves are largely mediated by our material possessions, from the clothes and jewelry we wear, to the cars we drive, to the houses we live in, or the churches in which we worship. Though external and in some ways superficial, material objects do say something about who we want to be and how we'd like to be perceived by others.

While different from Catholic priests wearing their white collars or nuns wearing habits, all material adornments offer cultural cues. So, what should we make of members of the clergy in other denominations whose external appearance seems no different from people on the street? Rick Warren, one of the most powerful evangelicals in the world, wears a Hawaiian shirt to preach. Is he hiding his true calling? Or, does he intentionally want to blend in with his congregation and with the wider culture in order to make everyone feel comfortable? Or perhaps he understands more clearly that collars and habits, crosses and rosaries, are relics whose outward showing may overshadow the underlying meaning of these objects? This may be another way to avoid idolatry (or even the appearance of it) and inspire deeper appreciation of how faith should be lived and expressed for some. Or more cynically, perhaps

Warren attracts more attention and members (and power) with his flagrant rejection of traditional priestly attire.

Material symbols of faith can be useful for the community as a means through which a set of beliefs are shared as well as communicated. In this light, the Ten Commandments are seen as rules of conduct whose relevance has not diminished since Moses' day. Religious people may ask, what is the problem with the display of this specific biblical relic on public land? The issue here, unlike wearing a cross on a necklace, is the separation between Church and State or more generally, the private and public domains, as laid down in the First Amendment of the Constitution and interpreted by the American judicial system. This means that one can do almost anything in the privacy of one's home as long as it doesn't hurt others, while in the public domain behavior is much more scrutinized and regulated. Since taxes are paid for the construction and maintenance of public spaces, in principle, citizens have the right to decide on what can or cannot happen there. As far as religious relics displayed on publicly funded land go, the First Amendment states:

> Congress shall make no law respecting an establishment of religion, or prohibiting the free exercise thereof; or abridging the freedom of speech, or of the press; or the right of the people peaceably to assemble, and to petition the Government for a redress of grievances.

The first part directly addresses what has been called the "Establishment Clause," according to which Congress cannot sanction a particular religion, such as Christianity, nor can there be any governmental restrictions on its free expression, as the second part asserts. Religious symbols and relics, then, can safely be presented within the confines of churches and in the homes of the faithful, but their placement in public spaces will be scrutinized, as the founders intended.

In many American churches, gone are the large gold statutes and prominent icons. In their stead, churches that now occupy large warehouse-like spaces are outfitted with minimal use of bells and smells. Recall that these modern acts of iconoclasm draw on a Calvinist heritage. This practice, though, is still bound by the context of

American capitalism: churches have to be built or warehouses have to be retrofitted; chairs have to be purchased and utilities have to be paid; administrators get paid and groundskeepers must water the lawn. Money has to be raised and donations collected. No matter the spiritual purpose behind such money matters, financial realities often occupy an inordinate amount of a church's attention. With this in mind, it's clear that the relics and iconography of the past may have left the Protestant church but have survived in different forms as a means for ensuring the operations of the modern church.

Relics in Religion and Sports

Expressions of wealth look the same whether we see them in ornate churches or gaudy mansions. The yardstick for success, then, looks similar in both secular and religious venues, even though there are great differences between the material and spiritual in principle. Obviously, it's difficult to see or measure one's inner peace of mind, one's love of God, and the sincerity of one's faith. Because of this difficulty, we can end up confusing the spiritual with the material, or trying to express the one through the other. The religious leader who is surrounded by material luxuries may *look* like a sports celebrity from the outside, but the expectation is that on the inside there *is* a difference between the two types of people. But is there? Both the religious leader and secular celebrity would claim that their success is expressed in similar ways because, in both cases, their true calling is being lived out and blessings presumably follow.

Tiger Woods made $75 million from May 2010 to May 2011, while Kobe Bryant made $53 million. Tennis legend Roger Federer made $47 million, and the European soccer star David Beckham $40 million during this same time frame. Some estimate that the Catholic Church's income in 2011 was more than $100 billion. Focus on the Family in Colorado Springs had revenues of around $116 million in 2010, while Lakewood Church, the mega-church in Houston, Texas pastored by Joel Osteen, collects about $75 million annually. These numbers are so large that they dwarf the kind of concerns that we may have with the pastor who merely owns an expensive car or takes a luxurious vacation. With such concentrated wealth, one wonders whether the means to accomplish religious work or the sacrifice athletes make are as relevant as they used to be when this kind of money wasn't involved. Are astronomical salaries justified in the case of athletes because their playing careers are so short? Or are they simply earning their market value? Likewise, is it necessary for churches to raise millions of dollars in order to perform their ministerial obligations? Can the amount of money become so great that it can only become the sole object of attention of a church? Money and what it can buy is not what pastors or athletes will claim motivates them. However, whether they like it or not, it is now perhaps the most important indicator of the value that society puts on their activities.

Ostentatious religious leaders and super-rich athletes are more than likely aware of these concerns and the judgment of hypocrisy that can be leveled against them. They would probably admit that to fetishize anything material is silly, sacrilegious, and unproductive. Likewise, they would more than likely assert that what is important is what is in their hearts and that they should be valued for what they do, how they conduct themselves, and what effects their behavior has in their community. None are delusional enough to believe that praying to a golden calf or holding superstitious beliefs will yield any results. But at times they betray their deeply held beliefs or so it seems from the outside. They seem to get caught up in the materialist culture in which they live, and lose sight of what they claim matters most—something spiritual.

While similarities exist between religion and sports as regards the expression of materialist desires, this does not mean that these expressions *necessarily* relate to each other. We have seen that relics have the power to motivate and guide action in both religion and sports, but baseball bats usually don't strengthen religious commitment. Yet certain relics from time to time have the power to bring sports and religion together and, in the process, reveal that the two can work in conjunction, not in competition, to draw out the power of the relic. The case of the "Bartman Ball" and its sacrifice-like destruction for the sake of the Chicago Cubs' fans and players illustrates our point well.

The streak of ninety-five disappointing seasons without a World Series championship for the Cubs nearly came to an end during the

2003 playoffs. The team needed a mere five outs to advance to their first World Series in almost 60 years. The Cubs were up 3–0 on the Florida Marlins in game six when the Marlins' Luis Castillo fouled off a ball toward the third base line. Cubs' left fielder Moises Alou ran toward the wall and reached into the stands to catch the ball for out number two, when a fan reached out as well deflecting Alou's glove from the ball. Alou immediately accosted the fan, Steve Bartman, for interfering with the play, which contributed, in however small way, to the eventual loss of the game and the series. Bartman was unfairly scapegoated and harassed by fans for months as the cause of the Cubs' demise. And the ball that Bartman touched immediately became a despised, but special relic that absorbed the anger of fans and players alike. It also became a material exhibit of the "Curse of the Billy Goat," a curse believed to have been placed on the Cubs by a disgruntled fan in 1947 that had somehow prevented a championship for the team.

Grant DePorter, a managing partner of the Harry Caray's Restaurant chain in Chicago, purchased the "Bartman Ball" at an auction from the fan who eventually ended up with it. His group paid a whopping $113,824 for the ball with the expressed intention of using it to somehow heal some of the fans' wounds. After taking fans' suggestions on what to do with the ball, he decided to destroy it in a public ceremony with the hope that it would lift the curse once and for all. The elaborate destruction of the ball, followed by the consumption of spaghetti sauce mixed with shards from the exploded orb gave the appearance of a classic sacrifice ritual. Along with the stated intentions that the event would mitigate the damage done by a fan (Bartman) to the Cubs' players by appeasing the "gods of the curse," we now have a full-fledged sacrificial ritual. Yet, we also can rightly suspect that DePorter had other, less religious intentions as well. While he probably did not consciously think that exploding the ball and including its remnants in the sauce was replicating an ancient sacrifice, on some level he knew that this act would help him earn a return on his hefty investment. With the media covering the destruction of the Bartman Ball and the remnants of what was left of the ball split up and displayed in all three of his restaurants, DePorter helped to ensure that this relic would pay off.

The Bartman Ball, then, is a sports relic that draws on religion to give itself added value from an unlikely source. While many fans may have thought that the annihilation of the ball only served a kind of sports purpose (it *may* enable the Cubs to win a World Series finally), it worked on some level because the ball carried some religious significance (Scholes 2005). The same can be said of the high financial value that DePorter placed on a ball (and perhaps recouped) that originally cost the team around $15. The fact that the ball was a sports relic that underwent a kind of religious ceremony has helped him recover some of the money spent.

This series of events prompts several questions and answers for us. As a relic, did the Bartman Ball serve an actual religious purpose? Yes, insofar as it was perceived, even unwittingly, to be a biblical-like offering that would lift the curse. Did it serve a financial purpose? Yes, insofar as the destruction of the ball and the display of its remnants have brought customers into the restaurant. Did it serve a sports purpose? Yes, insofar as it brought back together fans and their sports team to some extent. Would the highly symbolic and extravagant destruction of a mere baseball disturb the God of the Bible and John Calvin alike? Yes, insofar as too much value was placed on a material object. Could the ball's value be considered a fetish according to Marx? Yes, insofar as it is a commodity in the first place *and* its price was hugely inflated.

It is in these questions and answers that we find the role of the relic coalescing in religion and sports. The relic, with its general function of carrying meaning that supersedes its mere materiality, brings together the ways that various institutions value objects. And in certain relics such as the Bartman Ball, we find it more and more difficult to figure out where religion ends and where the value that fans and players place on sports relics begins. As with the cross worn around a neck or a special baseball, the religious and secular inform each other and cooperate, not necessarily compete, to convey the power that still exerts itself in a capitalistic, postsecular society regarding relics of all kinds. Contemporary consumer culture makes it easy to confuse an over-arching fetish-like relationship that we have with our commodities described by Marx with the reverence that is shown to material objects that have spiritual value.

Capitalism also blurs the line between the pursuit of success through wealth gain followed by churches and sports teams alike. A postsecular perspective on the matter allows us to retain the differences in their respective goals while admitting that the methods used to attain success often bear a strong resemblance. Both religion and sports are embedded in a capitalistic culture, after all. Therefore, it is the expectation that relics from religion and sports will be radically different that is rarely met in today's society. There may be confusion about the status of relics and what warrants their use in some cases and not in others. This confusion, however, does not mean that sports relics are reducible to religious ones or vice versa, but instead that the endowment of both kinds of relics with added value may, in fact, be drawing on a similar cultural source.

4

PILGRIMAGE

In a sense, we are all on a journey or a pilgrimage of sorts. A life consists in experiencing a series of events, both important and mundane, that often seem to be teaching us a lesson, even transforming us in some ways, as we are led to a destination. Getting into the college of our choice is a transformational process with a clear destination. Perhaps seeing one's children and grandchildren be successful is what one's life is geared towards. Or in the case of the Pilgrims in American history, the desire was to experience freedom from a repressive king where the destination was a new land across the Atlantic Ocean. If cast in a religious light, the destination is more than likely an ultimate "place" such as enlightenment, salvation, full consciousness, or a final union with the divine.

As such, a pilgrimage, in a religious sense, is more than a trip or a journey that only has its sights set on reaching a final destination. It is as much about the way one gets there as it is about the "there." What the idea of a pilgrimage suggests is that acquiring religious or spiritual truth is not easy or instant. The ritualistic quality of a pilgrimage requires the traveler to pass through different stages, endure trials, and change in the process in order to arrive at the destination. Clearly, belief and sacrifice play a role in the pilgrimage too, as the gratification that comes with its accomplishment is neither certain to come nor quick and painless. Often, a part of the pain that accompanies a pilgrimage involves physical hardship that attends the traversing of vast geographical distances and subjecting oneself to the deprivation of basic needs. If a journey does not involve the difficult crossing of certain thresholds along the way, it may merely be a trip, but not a pilgrimage. In addition, unlike the uneasy relationship between material relics and spiritual truth in many religious traditions, religious pilgrimages usually *require* materiality in the form of visceral discomfort and physical landmarks to make them work. If the avoiding of idolatry demands the distancing of materiality from God, pilgrimages can close this distance by demanding ritualistic physical action and adversity in order to reach spiritual goals.

Pilgrimages, though, do not always entail traveling through time and space to arrive at a physical destination. Akin to the terminology used when discussing sacrifice, instead of relying on *external* milestones to mark progress in a pilgrimage, one can go on an *internal* pilgrimage that takes place within oneself. Instead of bodily changes that necessarily occur on external pilgrimages, here, changes are psychological, emotional, or spiritual and can happen without ever leaving the confines of one's room. But in the end, many spiritual or internal pilgrimages are no less grueling or able to generate real success than those that require sweat.

Pilgrimage in the Bible

Early humans in hunter-gatherer societies went on a kind of pilgrimage daily in order to locate plentiful food and hunt game. In ancient religions that followed the hunter-gatherer age but developed in more settled, agricultural communities, we see a different kind of pilgrimage that transcended the acquisition of the basics for survival (the goal in hunter-gatherer communities)—the goal began to be *spiritual* in nature. For instance, the "vision quest" is an old rite of passage in many Native American religions where a boy or girl must enter the woods alone for a period of time with the purpose of leaving as a man or woman. To attain the spiritual awareness necessary to facilitate this transition, one must fast and meditate, as these activities are believed to bring closer the spirits needed to shepherd the transition.

Pilgrimages are present in all of the major world religions as well. Many Hindus have shrines to gods inside their homes. However, they also practice their cherished rite of pilgrimage by leaving the comforts of home to visit rivers, temples, and mountains where gods are believed to reside. Buddhists, while relying primarily on meditation to achieve enlightenment or nirvana, are instructed by the Buddha to make pilgrimages to several of the important places in the Buddha's life. Just as the Buddha set out on the pilgrimage that changed his life as a young man, he made clear that his followers needed to retrace his footsteps in order to gain a sense of spiritual urgency that could not be felt in one's hometown or village. Muhammad valued pilgrimage so highly that he required traveling to Mecca at least one time in the life of a Muslim (the *Hajj*) as one of the five Pillars of Islam. Bolstered by the pilgrimage of Abraham to Mecca, Muhammad's own pilgrimage from the city of Medina to his hometown of Mecca is to be repeated by all Muslims. Muhammad's trek that ends with the monumental destruction of the idols of the tribal religions reveals the truth (first revealed to Abraham) of worshipping only one God to the Meccans. Muslims are commanded, if physically and financially able, to repeat Muhammad's journey and spend 12 days fasting, praying, and experiencing the solidarity and equality of all present.

The Bible is replete with examples of pilgrimages and their pilgrims. One could interpret the ejection of Adam and Eve from Eden by God as the beginning of a life-long pilgrimage for all of humanity. Later in the Hebrew Bible, we see Jacob, grandson of the patriarch Abraham, setting off on a pilgrimage after being sent away by his father, Isaac. Indentured servitude, famine, placing conditions on God, and even a wrestling match with an angel punctuate his journey. But Jacob keeps his faith in the covenant that God made with his people, and after living in Egypt with his family to escape a famine, he dies and his corpse is returned home, thus completing his pilgrimage.

The most significant pilgrimage in the Bible is the exodus led by Moses—the collective migration of the Israelites out of slavery in Egypt to the Promised Land in modern-day Israel. They wandered for

40 years in the desert of the Arabian peninsula with little food or water and armed with only their faith that God, through his prophet Moses, would deliver on the promise. It is a pilgrimage *par excellence* because it possesses the twin themes of the external and the internal. The Israelites knew from Moses that the Promised Land was the goal of their pilgrimage but were far from certain whether they would ever get there. The lack of food (external) and anxiety over whether Moses was to be trusted (internal) makes this journey a classic pilgrimage. Even though they did not always realize this along the way, they eventually believed that God was watching over them and guiding them to their destination. And according to the narrative, when they finally arrived in Canaan, the promise fulfilled served to justify the suffering, both physical and psychological, endured.

In the New Testament, as with most religious concepts and themes that we cover in this book, there is a shift in the language and the appearance of a pilgrimage. According to the Gospel accounts, Jesus went on a classic pilgrimage of sorts when he ventured out for 40 days and nights in the desert to fast and pray before being tempted by the devil to accept food and power, but to no avail. Yet Jesus does not ask his disciples to mimic this type of pilgrimage, practiced as well by John the Baptist, where one must abscond to the desert to experience spiritual truths. Indeed, Jesus promotes the very act of following him as a pilgrimage in and of itself, which entails a physical and spiritual tracing of his footsteps, though not to the desert. Jesus says to his disciples:

> Anyone who loves their father or mother more than me is not worthy of me; anyone who loves their son or daughter more than me is not worthy of me. Whoever does not take up their cross and follow me is not worthy of me.
>
> (Matthew 10:37–38)

The ultimate goal of the Christian pilgrimage, then, is salvation, and many Christians believe that the *only* way to get there is to follow Jesus alone, as seems to be expressed in John 14:6. To the disciples, on one level, he actually meant walk behind me and imitate me, which necessarily entailed leaving one's family. On another level, later generations of Christians have interpreted this command as a metaphorical following of Jesus—the actual leaving of a family is not necessary to be a Christian, but the honoring of Jesus above one's mother and father is.

A different kind of pilgrimage that is also privileged in the New Testament emphasizes the spreading of the Gospel good news to those who have not heard it. Here, the goal of any such pilgrimage is the conversion of others and not necessarily the attainment of spiritual truth or personal salvation, though saving of others is the primary way in which the Kingdom will be made manifest, according to many Christians. When the disciples were sent out by Jesus to preach the good news, he demanded that they set out without money, "Do not get any gold or silver or copper to take with you in your belts," and warned them of hardships that they would face: "you will be handed over to the local councils and be flogged in the synagogues" (Matthew 10:9, 17). Suffering and even death could be expected. Paul, who was not one of the twelve disciples of Jesus but a later convert, accepts this charge to evangelize by going on mission-journeys to convert Gentiles. Just as Jesus warned, Paul endures imprisonment, torture, and likely death as the price paid for the spreading of Jesus' message, at least as Paul interprets this treatment. In his second letter to the Corinthians, he remarks:

> We are afflicted in every way, but not crushed; perplexed, but not driven to despair; persecuted, but not forsaken; struck down, but not destroyed; always carrying in the body the death of Jesus, so that the life of Jesus may also be made visible in our bodies.
> (2 Corinthians 12:8–10)

The main difference seen in these Christian mission-pilgrimages is the recognition of the external and the internal, not as mutually intertwined, but as parallel journeys. Earlier, the external, as expressed in the journey to the Promised Land, was an integral part of the internal: the struggle to maintain faith. With Jesus' disciples and Paul, the mission-pilgrimage is not necessarily the means to realize the true end of salvation—it is what one should do *after* one is saved. Salvation, in the most general Christian sense, is the end of *another* kind of pilgrimage: one that has little to do with obeying the Law or putting forth human effort of any kind. It is an internal pilgrimage that requires the belief that Jesus' own pilgrimage to the cross is efficacious and sufficient. Hence, in Christianity, there seem to be two kinds of pilgrimages: the *external* mission pilgrimage meant to bring salvation to others, and the *internal* spiritual journey meant to save the soul.

In later Christian writings on pilgrimages, mission work is still important, but the internal pilgrimage is highlighted more often. In John Bunyan's classic, *The Pilgrim's Progress*, written in 1678, the reader is taken on the pilgrimage of a man named Christian. Christian travels from a mythical "City of Destruction" to the "Celestial City." He deals with trials along the way, as one would on any pilgrimage, on his way to the goal. But Bunyan's protagonist is dealing primarily with internal struggles, such as the reckoning with his own sinful life, and the Celestial City is really in his own mind. Upon arrival, he realizes that his sins have been forgiven by Jesus' sacrifice. Any reader can mimic a Christian's pilgrimage—not by reaching a holy site or trekking out to the desert, but by repenting for a sinful life.

It is the internal pilgrimage that is prominent in Christianity to this day. While the external pilgrimage of mission work is still respected and engaged by some, the modern Christian most often believes that she can gain salvation without venturing out and risking death, as the early Christians did. Despite this shift, the markings of the classic religious pilgrimage (setting out, living with uncertainty, struggling with hardships, maintaining faith, and reaching the goal) still hold significance in our collective imagination as we admire those who embark on external pilgrimages to help guide their internal journey. Whether Jerusalem or Mecca, Plymouth Rock or the Salt Lake in Utah, these destinations mark the end of historic pilgrimages that still resonate and can, at times, be translated into fruitful internal pilgrimages today for the modern American pilgrim.

Pilgrimage in Sports

Pilgrimages may not immediately come to mind when thinking about sports. True, an athlete embarks on a journey when he or she decides to pursue a lofty goal, such as a gold medal or a career as a professional athlete. But, unlike famous religious figures, one would be hard-pressed to find the word "pilgrimage" in stories about successful athletes. Yet in spite of the lack of explicit pilgrimage language in "athlete-speak" or sports commentary, if we remember the general qualities of a pilgrimage, we will find many of these qualities in sports.

As with belief, sacrifice, and relics, the different ways that a pilgrimage is expressed in sports breaks down along the line between athletes and fans. And using the conceptual framework that we used to describe pilgrimages found in the Bible, the sports pilgrimage also tends to be both internal and external. The athlete's pilgrimage may or may not have a clear finish line, and hence the external is sometimes downplayed in relation to the internal journey that often involves self-doubt, anxiety, frustration, and hopefully extreme self-satisfaction. For the fan, if a sports-related pilgrimage is undertaken, it tends to be guided by external, material features rather than internal, spiritual/psychological ones as the destination is often a special physical building in a special place.

As we mentioned in Chapter 2, athletes must sacrifice much in order to be successful. Recall that the truly successful athlete, from an early age, must often forego the comforts of sleep, diet, and a normal social life. Each self-denying action is a sacrifice itself, but in order for each small sacrifice to be worth it, it must fit into a bigger picture in the life of the athlete. If sacrifices, as well as the triumphs that follow, are situated in the wider context of a long-term pilgrimage, the struggles encountered can be more easily justified and surmounted. Conversely, if a particular hardship is not part of a journey that is oriented to a bigger goal, even the most talented athlete can be undone by a single instance of suffering.

In the case of Houston Rockets point guard Jeremy Lin, we see a classic sports pilgrimage that has played out in his career that expresses this dynamic. Lin, a 6-foot 3-inch Taiwanese American, was never told that he could make it in the NBA. This is due in part to his ethnicity—very few Asians have ever suited up in the league—and therefore, Lin was not taken seriously as a young player. Despite making the All-State team in California his senior year of high school, no Division I college actively recruited him. After finishing a stellar career at Harvard, both on the court and in the classroom, Lin went undrafted in the 2010 NBA draft. He was eventually signed by an NBA team that promptly cut him after one season. He was signed by another team only to be cut two weeks later. The New York Knicks then signed him, and a couple of days from being cut again and sleeping on a friend's couch the night before a game, Lin finally got his chance to play. He took full advantage of the opportunity, leading the Knicks to seven straight wins and solidifying his role as the new starting point guard in the 2011–2012 season. This string of performances helped land him a long-term and lucrative contract with the Houston Rockets in the summer of 2012.

Facing incredible odds, Lin found success because he has *always* been on a kind of pilgrimage. His destination for the longest time was simply to make it to the NBA. This dream enabled the overcoming of major obstacles and self-doubt. Even though his next goal is likely a championship—a measurable, tangible goal such as making the NBA—Lin and most other top-level athletes experience their pilgrimages internally too. Lin locates his basketball journey within the context of an internal spiritual journey as he revealed in 2012:

> I will always, always have doubters, but I really want to reach my potential to bring glory to God. That is more motivation than haters and doubters. I want to work just as hard, give just as much, whether or not I have haters.

Dealing with the uncertainty, using the doubters' comments as motivation, picking yourself up after rejection and failure—all are elements that the athlete-as-pilgrim must reckon with on his or her own.

Unlike a personal pilgrimage that is merely a component of success in some sports, there are other sports that are actually pilgrimages in themselves. Three prominent, but not exhaustive, examples are mountaineering, cycling, and long-distance running. In mountaineering, climbers prepare for months and years before they can undertake the arduous travails and risk their lives in order to reach the highest peaks, such as K2 (28,251 feet) and of course, Mount Everest (29,029 feet). In cycling, the most famous of all races is the Tour de France—an annual endurance race that covers 2,200 miles and takes three weeks to complete. In long-distance running, a marathon is the classic yardstick by which runners from around the world best the other runners' times to complete the 26.2 mile course. In all of these cases, the race *is* the pilgrimage—a onetime test of commitment, willingness to sacrifice, stamina, and determination. Athletes competing in these races experience both the uncertainty and the dangers that accompany any pilgrimage, and accordingly, success in these three sports is possible because an inner strength separates the winners from the losers.

The fan, on the other hand, may embark on a sports pilgrimage, but an internal struggle is less present as it is an external milestone that invites the journey. Like the Catholic who makes a pilgrimage to the Vatican or the Muslim who travels to Mecca, many sports fans make it a lifetime goal to visit their cherished sports shrines. Most obvious are the historic stadiums, such as Fenway Park in Boston or Lambeau Field in Green Bay, Wisconsin. These are stadiums that were built at a time when their respective sports, baseball and football, were just beginning. Like Jerusalem for pilgrims of the three great monotheisms, these stadiums are points of origin. Moreover, unlike entering a brand new, often glitzy stadium, walking into an old building is like traveling back in time and through space to a purer, simpler day. Some ambitious fans participate in a series of pilgrimages that encompass one grand pilgrimage by making sure they see *every* ballpark in the United States at some point in their lives. More costly in terms of time and money, these pilgrimages act as an homage to an entire sport rather than to a single team's stadium.

Halls of Fame are single buildings dedicated to honoring the greatest in a single sport. They invite the sports pilgrim to step back in time in a different way than the historic stadium does. The Pro Football Hall of Fame in Canton, Ohio; the National Baseball Hall of Fame in Cooperstown, New York; and the Naismith Basketball Hall of Fame in Springfield, Massachusetts; to name a few, are the destinations of thousands of fans each year. Their location in small towns instead of big cities lend a feel to the pilgrimage not wholly unlike an ascetic's trip to a remote desert—it takes more effort and deliberation to travel to these sites than it typically would to a large metropolis, and one can expect less of a frenetic pace in these locations than is found in big cities. And like many sacred shrines, Halls of Fame are filled with relics, such as famous balls, pucks, and uniforms, which stand as material reminders of the sports "gods" and "saints" who used them. Artificial light emanates from the edges of bronze busts of the NFL Hall of Famers on display that lends an almost ethereal (holy?) feel to the men depicted in the sculptures. Some stadiums close the distance between the shrine dedicated to their legendary players and the playing field itself by containing them in one venue. Yankee Stadium, though a 2009 replica of the original, has its "Monument Park" in right field, which contains plaques and the retired numbers of the legendary Yankees chosen to grace its space.

Pilgrimages to stadiums and Halls of Fame may not involve deep internal doubt or require intestinal fortitude for the pilgrim. In fact, many visit these sites every year without any inkling that these spaces are sacred to others. Hence for the pilgrim trekking to certain stadiums or Halls of Fame, these spaces hold a heightened significance, but like the uninterested visitor, an internal struggle may not have to be involved to arrive at these locations. The sports shrine focuses the fan's attention largely on the external—distant geographical locations, material buildings, and their contents. But these are pilgrimages nonetheless in that a fan must at least leave the relative comfort of home and make some sacrifices in the form of time and money in order to finally arrive at the sacred destination.

Returning to the athlete for a moment, we are reminded that even though his or her pilgrimage demands internal fortitude, there is often a strong external element as well. The major American sports, both professional and collegiate, do not have a set location for their championships; it usually changes each year. In these sports, it is the championship alone, despite the place in which it happens, that marks the end of an athlete's or team's pilgrimage. In other sports, such as tennis and golf, there are major tournaments each year that take place at the same location. Therefore, the aspiring tennis or golf star's pilgrimage has as its ultimate end a championship that is inextricably linked with the physical site at which it takes place. The grass courts of Wimbledon in England, the dirt on the track of the Kentucky Derby, the fully bloomed azaleas at Augusta National golf course, the skyscraper-lined route of the New York marathon, or the black asphalt of the Indianapolis 500—all cannot be separated from the dream of hoisting the trophy at the end.

The Olympics occupy a space between the moving location of the Super Bowl and the fixed location of tennis' French Open. Yes, the summer and winter Olympics are given to different cities each time, but because they occur every four years, hopeful athletes certainly set their sights, for instance, on Nagano, Japan in 1998 and Sochi, Russia in 2014. The Olympic pilgrim must shift attention to the next site after the games are over, but four years is plenty of time to establish a new pilgrimage to the upcoming location. Indeed, a symbolic pilgrimage takes place before each Olympic games as a torch lit by an eternal flame in Athens, Greece is transported mostly by land to the host city. Viewers are invited to identify with the various runners carrying the torch and to follow the single flame as it goes on its own pilgrimage, often through rough terrain and inclement weather.

In all of the examples presented above, whether it be the athlete's solitary, internal journey or the fan's trip across the country to a physical shrine, sports clearly offers its own distinct version of a pilgrimage. There may be varying degrees of hardship and uncertainty depending on whether one is an athlete or fan as well as varying types of destinations. But no less than the religious pilgrimages, these sports pilgrimages contain the necessary qualities of the kind of journey that can be transformative.

Pilgrimage and Religion Today

When we think of a pilgrimage in terms of an external–internal dynamic, it helps us see more clearly the way in which pilgrimages intersect with religion today but only by first putting modern pilgrimages into the context of certain historical pilgrimages. One that occurred in an American context is the journey undertaken by Mormon pioneers in the middle of the nineteenth century. Their journey took them from the Northeast through the Midwest to finally settle in the Great Basin in Utah. Having endured the only extinction order ever handed down by the United States government, the constant fear of attack from neighbors, and the assassination of their founder,

Joseph Smith, the Mormons' trek ended on a high note with 70,000 strong landing in what would become the Utah Territory beginning in 1847. The overall journey that started in 1838 and ended in 1869 has been labeled the "Mormon Exodus." Just as the Israelites left Egypt because of persecution, so did the Mormons; just as the Israelites arrived at their Promised Land and built the temple in Jerusalem, so did the Mormons arrive and build their own temple in Salt Lake City.

The theme of the pilgrimage that is initiated by religious persecution and finds relief in new territories that are more hospitable has been echoed for centuries in all major religions. This theme still resonates today because it makes visible—moving from one place to another (external journey)—what remains invisible for many on their own pilgrimage—God's plan and the blessing that reveals that plan (internal journey). This seeking for a divine plan and the destination believed to be laid out by God is itself a pilgrimage, but what has changed between the America of two centuries ago and the present is the appreciation that seeking is not just a means to another end but is now an end in itself. Robert Wuthnow explains changes in spiritual practices in this way:

> [A] traditional spirituality of inhabiting sacred places has given way to a new spirituality of seeking. [Americans] negotiate more among competing views of the sacred, seeking partial knowledge and practical wisdom . . . spirituality of dwelling emphasizes *habitation*: God occupies a definite place in the universe and creates a sacred space in which humans too can dwell; to inhabit sacred space is to know its territory and to feel secure. A spirituality of seeking emphasizes *negotiation*: individuals search for sacred moments that reinforce their conviction that the divine exists, but these moments are fleeting; rather than knowing the territory, people explore new spiritual vistas, and they may have to negotiate among complex and confusing meanings of spirituality.
> (Wuthnow 1998, 3–4)

Because the sacred, in a postsecular sense, is infused with the secular, the boundaries that used to mark off the sacred and allow for "dwelling" there may not be as obvious as they used to be nor as inhabitable. If the sacred is much more difficult to find today, then seeking may never really end, and all we can hope for at the "end" of a religious pilgrimage is "partial knowledge and practical [not metaphysical] knowledge." Consequently, the physicality or materiality of a sacred space, a temple or shrine, a city, or rock formation that can be touched, occupied, and even inhabited by the "dweller" has become less needed in facilitating the spiritual journey of the seeker. Moreover, the inwardness associated with seeking blurs the boundaries separating the sacred and secular and, therefore, one no longer has to reach a particular destination—salvation can be found wherever and under whatever conditions one lives in.

As Wuthnow continues to explain, the activity of seeking cannot be separated from consumer culture, which honors the seeking that precedes the purchase of an item above all else. Religion itself has become another commodity to the extent that its own boundaries, historically associated with the sacred, have become less distinct in relation to other, more commercial commodities. As noted in our Introduction, competition between the sacred and the secular assumes that there is a strict separation between the two. And "For a time, the religion industry competed mainly with secular ideas and activities for the energy of consumers" (Ibid., 12). But now, without a strict separation between religion and secularity in the postsecular market-place for the seeker, real competition has ceased as well.

> In recent decades, however, the religion industry itself has experienced a significant expansion, and the boundaries between it and other industries have become blurred. Publishers, thera-pists, independent authors, and spiritual guides of all kinds have entered the marketplace. It is not surprising, therefore, that people shop for spirituality and that they do so in an increasing variety of ways.
>
> (Ibid., 12)

And one of the ways that religion is "purchased" is in the form of a kind of commercialized pilgrimage now sold in the form of travel packages to tourists. In 2011 close to 3.5 million people visited the Holy Land as tourists and more than half of them were Christians. One of the more popular outfits, Holy Land Tours, promotes its trips in the following way:

> Join us on a ten day spiritual journey focusing on the Life and times of Jesus, "walking where Jesus walked." Imagine yourself in the Galilee, and in Capernaum—referred as Jesus "own town" (Matthew 9:1), where Jesus began his ministry (Mark 1:21, John 6:59), and recruited his first disciple (John 21:15–17). Stand on the Mt. of Beatitudes (Matthew 5, Matthew 6, Matthew 7, Matthew 8) and make believe you are listening to the Lord preach the Sermon on the Mount. Submerge yourself in the Jordan River, where Jesus was baptized by John the Baptist (John 1:29–33). Continue on to the Golden City of Jerusalem, and walk the Stations of the Cross on the Via Dolorosa, where you can take time to reflect the Lord's sacrifice for all of us, and what an incredible moment it will be when you stand on the Mt. of Olives in Jerusalem, where Jesus ascended in to heaven (Acts 1). We invite you not just on another trip, but a spiritual journey you will never forget.
>
> (www.holylandtourstravel.com)

As it says, this is not just "another trip, but a spiritual journey." Here, the pilgrimage language is evident—walking in the footsteps of Jesus does not just present the beauty of the area or an overwhelming feeling of the historic significance of the land, but a spiritual experience.

What this blurb leaves out is that tourists will stay in a "5 Star Deluxe Hotel" where nice meals will be provided daily. So while tourists/pilgrims mimic the pilgrimage of Jesus and his disciples, their retreat to luxurious accommodations looks more like a pleasure vacation to a beachside resort than a difficult journey. The boundaries between the two kinds of trips have, as Wuthnow says, indeed become blurred. However, the pilgrimage aspect of these trips is the real reason for this trip, yet we can certainly question whether tourists walking the Stations of the Cross are experiencing the requisite hardship to equate it to Jesus' pilgrimage on the same path 2,000 years ago.

As the website promotes, it is a spiritual journey that is accomplished through the visiting of an actual holy destination. So here we have more of an internal pilgrimage that is achieved by virtue of a kind of external journey, albeit less strenuous than it could be. But given the way in which the sacred and secular come together more seamlessly today than in times past, then combined with an emphasis on the internal journey over an external one, it should not trouble us too much if these trips are labeled "pilgrimages" either by the companies that sell them or by the participants who fork out the money to take them.

It is possible nowadays to remove the external portion of a pilgrimage to the Holy Land altogether while still retaining some of the qualities of a pilgrimage. Countless websites offer virtual tours of the Holy Land, walking tours of Jerusalem, and sightseeing in Rome. Your own avatar can "walk" through narrow alleys and "visit" the sacred places, "sit" within the ruins, "stand" right where religious saints stood centuries ago, and "pray" with them. Technology allows for contemporary seekers the convenience of roaming through a virtual reality for a small fee without ever having to leave their bedroom. The authenticity of some of these tours is sanctioned by religious organizations and the accuracy of what one is seeing on a computer screen is confirmed by expert virtual tour guides. Yes, your avatar is walking through the Holy Land, but are you? Does your avatar actually see, smell, and touch the landmarks along the way? Is seeing the sights through a computer screen similar to seeing them in person? The external component of these pilgrimages is largely removed, though not eliminated altogether, so if any kind of journey is embarked on at all in one of these virtual tours, perhaps it is more of an internal, spiritual journey. Yet absent the external landmarks shown on a computer screen, would the spiritual journey be as profound without them?

The point of the religious pilgrimage is to bring the external and the internal together in a balanced way: the one is appreciated through the other. Just as the shopping mall has not been completely replaced by the virtual mall (yet), so have sacred spaces and churches not been completely replaced by inner spirituality. Religious faith, sacrifice, iconography, and pilgrimage today may be less bound by specific biblical injunctions and bricks-and-mortar institutions, but this doesn't mean that they have completely lost their meaning and significance. Though transformed in the era of consumer society and the Internet, their power as symbols remains intact. And because of their symbolic power, they continue to assert a certain authority over believers in all religions. This authority demands a level of sophistication that pushes individuals to reflect on their actions when following the rules and regulations of religious doctrines. Reflection is needed because reliable external cues, such as parting of the Red Sea or hearing God's voice at Mount Sinai, are largely unavailable in today's pilgrimage. It is because of this, rather than despite it, that we find more profound examples of internal journeys that fulfill the expectation of a full-blown pilgrimage. And these pilgrimages can be just as demanding and difficult, requiring a level of reflection and selflessness the harshness of which is impossible to measure and at times attain.

Wuthnow describes this shift from spiritual dwellers to seekers as a process by which religious pilgrims no longer have to land in traditional spaces, such as churches or shrines. Nor do they have to rely on material symbols, such as the Torah scroll for Jews or the cross for Christians. Questioning all of their traditional sacred places and symbols, seekers, though, are charged with coming up with their own definitions and means of understanding, with reconfiguring them from a multitude of sources, and finally generating what they deem to be authentic religious experiences.

Pilgrimage in Religion and Sports

Instead of spending money to take a tour of the Holy Land and be pampered in air-conditioned hotels, St. Francis of Assisi (1181–1286) began his own pilgrimage by giving up all worldly possessions and living a life of poverty, as he believed Jesus called him to do. As strange as it may seem, perhaps our closest analog to St. Francis today is the soldier who gives up much for a bigger cause or the athlete who foregoes physical and social comfort to train each morning. Yet, in the latter's case, when an athlete makes millions of dollars to compensate for the hard work, a figure like St. Francis still seems far away.

One could argue that the tourist pilgrimage, whether to a sacred place, a national park, or a hallowed place in sports history, has replaced the long, arduous ones found in religious history. Stadiums and Halls of Fame are some of the new sacred spaces that invite Americans of all stripes to set out on a significant journey, so the argument goes. But have sports shrines and similar secular destinations *replaced* the religious shrine for the modern day pilgrim's attention? Or is it more appropriate to think of the sports pilgrimage as *displacing* the traditional religious pilgrimage on the face of it, while allowing the religious/spiritual character of a pilgrimage to inform and even guide the fan? Likewise, can we honor the effort put forth in the athlete's pilgrimage while resisting the temptation to compare it to religious pilgrimages where the pilgrim encounters life-and-death dangers?

Regarding the fan's pilgrimage in the case of baseball, David Chidester writes that the sport does many of the things that religion does, thus effectively blurring the lines between the religious and secular components of a pilgrimage to a baseball shrine. He writes, "baseball ensures a sense of continuity in the midst of a constantly changing America through the forces of tradition, heritage, and collective memory." It also "supports a sense of uniformity, a sense of belonging to a vast, extended American family that attends the same church." And finally, the "religion of baseball represents the sacred space of home. In this respect, baseball is a religion of the domestic, of the familiar . . ." (Chidester 1996, 745–746). Given that, for Chidester, baseball functions as the "sacred space of home," it stands to reason that a pilgrimage can be seen as a sacred trip home. In fact, Muhammad's pilgrimage to Mecca was really a trip back to his hometown, as Muslims believe that they, too, are going home when they go on the *Hajj*. In addition, the parable of the prodigal son found in the Gospel according to Luke is really about a son's journey home.

What Chidester does is displace, not replace, the historical religious language we have come to expect when describing the "church" and/or the "sacred." By likening baseball stadiums to places of worship and home with the sacred functionally, Chidester can use sports to talk about a religious pilgrimage. This is not a sleight of hand in which he substitutes baseball as a brand new religion that pushes out the older, institutional religion, nor are sports pilgrimages replacing religious ones. Instead, the very process of *seeking* is infiltrated by the sacred and, at times, finds it in sports as a kind of home without home being a final destination.

We see this kind of pilgrimage being played out in some American cultural expressions. The movie, "Field of Dreams," (1989) condenses several spiritual pilgrimages into one movie that is about baseball, at least on the surface. The main character, Ray Kinsella, while struggling financially in rural Iowa, hears voices telling him "if you build it, he will come" and "go the distance." He reluctantly disregards the protests of his wife and responds to the voices by building a baseball diamond in the middle of a cornfield. Players from a long-gone team miraculously emerge from the corn field to play, though Ray is the only one who can see them at first. Each player is a kind of time-traveling pilgrim beckoned by Ray's constructed sacred space. Ray himself is on a pilgrimage too, as the "he" in "if you build it, he will come" refers to his deceased father who appears in spirit form on the home plate of the field at the end of the movie. Instead of the "he" being God, as one may expect, it is really his dad. And instead of God speaking to Ray, it is the voice of a deceased ballplayer. Instead of redemption being found inside the walls of a church and through divine revelation, it is found on the field through the playing of the game itself in its original, organic, and pastoral setting. And instead of a pilgrimage that ends with the reunion with his dad in heaven, Ray's pilgrimage starts and ends at home.

Whether chronicled in movies or in the Bible or experienced in the weight room or through a computer screen, a pilgrimage remains a steadfast means to ground a search for meaning or for a destination. It also can elevate the significance of mundane activities such as staying after practice shooting jump shots or meditating each morning because these activities are situated in a moving stream that is heading for a grander goal. The reluctance to relate the religious pilgrimage to the sports pilgrimage may occur today because the goals of each seem so different. But are they? Since the religious pilgrimage for many Americans has largely gone internal and is characterized primarily by a perpetual seeking for partial answers that commercial interests can easily prey on, it barely resembles that of the ancient Israelites or of Jesus' disciples. In fairness, nor does the pilgrimage of the athlete, yet the language used to covey both types of pilgrimage is similar. Today, both the language *and* the action in the religious and sports pilgrimage can be more easily used to reinforce the other as participants in each domain embark on journeys that may have different goals but are able to fulfill similar functions for the pilgrim.

5

COMPETITION

Competition often gets a bad rap in our culture. In fact, pianist Glenn Gould is reputed to have said that the root of all evil isn't money, it's competition (Hubeart 1996). Competition is sometimes thought of as inherently selfish and damaging to all involved when it is often contrasted with the kinder, gentler act of cooperation. To cooperate is to help another achieve a common goal as they help you too; to compete, in most cases, is to attempt to eliminate the other from the competition so the goal can be reached by you alone.

We are all too familiar with the over-competitive father who pushes his son or daughter to unreasonable lengths in academics or sports or the politician who uses a "whatever it takes" strategy to beat an opponent. Certainly competition or competitiveness can be taken too far. However, it is also an essential feature of life without which the human race would remain relatively stagnant. It is competition that drives a restaurant to raise the quality of its food over the restaurant down the street. It is competition with fellow students that pushes the pre-med undergraduate to study for five hours a day thus becoming a better doctor down the road. It is competition that compels states to fight for federal dollars to improve their public schools. It is competition with the old Soviet Union that helped the United States defeat communism. And on the most basic level of all, it is competition between species that is the engine of evolution. Competition often takes place because there is a limited amount of desired resources to supply what we need and want. We must compete with those seeking the same resources because of their scarcity.

In addition, competition is primarily social. Though a person may compete with his or her own time in marathons or one's own golf handicap, more often than not, competition involves more than one person. And it being social, there are several ways that competition puts people into relationship with each other. In a zero-sum game, the winner of a competition wins at the expense of the loser. Or, all competitors cannot benefit or alternatively, lose. This kind of competition has obvious advantages in that it rewards the better competitor and can motivate the one who lost to try to acquire the benefits the next time around. However, a zero-sum competition has its drawbacks, too. How are we to think of the third world country that cannot feasibly compete with a first world country for money and resources? Should the citizens of the losing country be forced to starve? Perhaps a winner-take-all game in geopolitics is not the one we should be playing.

Another type of competition is that which motivates all parties to do their best, whether in the marketplace or on the sports field. In these cases, being competitive does not result in the inevitable loss but in the collective betterment of all competitors. You compete against others, but you also know that the better they become, the better you become in the process. Here, competition usually will not be completed at the end point of a tournament or war, and hence it can continually push the parties to improve as happens among members of the same team. For instance, the American auto industry on the whole has made significant improvements in the quality of its automobiles over the last several years in part *because* of competition between companies even when some companies were "losing." Yes, one company will always make more than others, but second place in this race only serves as motivation to improve, not as a reason to throw in the towel. Competition, whether in a winner-and-losers form or a winners-and-winners form, is an unavoidable aspect of American life, and as such, plays a major role in the ways in which religion and sports express themselves in culture.

Competition in the Bible

Competition is certainly not the first thing that comes to mind when pondering religion. For one, many religions emphasize the individual, solitary path to enlightenment or salvation, so competition with anyone else does not come into play. In addition, God is believed by most to be infinite and is therefore not a scarce resource—all can "have" God without fear that God will "run out." And finally, the kind of competition in which there are winners (the strong) and losers (the weak) runs counter to what we normally think of as a religious way of thinking about humanity. Jesus said that "the meek shall inherit the earth;" the meek might not survive a generation in Darwin's world.

Though in the Bible there is little time wasted in recounting an example of competition. Cain and Abel, the sons of Adam and Eve, took on different roles. Abel shepherded a flock, and Cain was a farmer. Each presented God with an offering, but God rejected Cain's offering while accepting Abel's. God notices Cain's distress over the divine favor curried with Abel and admonishes Cain for being a sore loser. Cain, presumably out of jealousy, calls Abel to a field where he kills him. When God asks Cain where his brother is, Cain famously replies, "Am I my brother's keeper?" and is later punished by being forced to wander the earth for his remaining days. We can see that Cain was competing with Abel for what turned out to be a limited resource—God's approval. It's possible that God could have accepted both offerings, but by rejecting Cain's, Abel suddenly became the winner. Getting Abel out of the way is undoubtedly one way of converting a loss into an ultimate victory, though Cain certainly loses in the end.

We see a similar sibling rivalry play out in the relationship between the twin sons of Isaac, Jacob and Esau. Esau was technically the first-born and was described as bigger, hairier, and more masculine than Jacob. Esau hunted; Jacob cooked food with his mother, Rebecca. When it came time for Isaac to give his blessing, a sacred honor given to the first-born son, Jacob, with the help of his mother, tricks his father into giving it to him instead. Esau was understandably upset and pleads to his father, "Have you not reserved a blessing for me?" Isaac responds, "I have already made him [Jacob] your lord, and I have given him all his brothers as servants, and with grain and wine I have sustained him. What then can I do for you, my son?" Esau replies plaintively, "Have you only one blessing, father? Bless me, me also father!" (Genesis 27:36–38). Clearly this is a zero-sum game with *extremely* limited resources. If Isaac was able to give Esau his birthright too, no competition between the brothers would have been necessary. But Jacob, albeit deceitfully, wins this competition handily while the refrain, "All's fair in love and war" should be in the backs of our minds. And unlike Cain's fate, Jacob's ill-gotten victory goes unpunished.

A competition of cosmic proportions takes place in the story of the Israelites' exodus from Egypt. The Pharaoh attempts to compete with the God of the Israelites by putting up his own magicians as competitors. Though it *appears* to be an even playing field between the two parties with the Pharaoh acting as the umpire for a while, this is no real competition, according to the story laid out in the book of Exodus. The magicians go toe-to-toe with God by replicating the first two of the nine plagues that God brings down on the Egyptians—God "hardens the Pharaoh's heart" so that stubbornness prevents him from letting the Israelites go for the remaining seven plagues. But the tenth and final plague, the wiping out of the first-born Egyptian males, is the undeniable proof that the God of the Israelites is too powerful for this competition to continue. The Pharaoh realizes that he and his magicians (and their gods) have been beaten. This story reveals that, one, God can have competition (recall that it is divulged in the second commandment that God is jealous); two, God is not beneath competing with others; and three, stories of competitive battles are great vehicles for transmitting theological truths to the faithful.

In the New Testament, while competition is not a common theme at all, it still serves as an important means for delivering spiritual truths. Jesus seems to have an ambivalent relationship with the idea of competition. At times he suggests that competition will not move one closer to God. For example, in his parable about laborers in a vineyard found in Matthew 20:1–16, some workers show up to work at 9:00 in the morning, some show up at noon, some at 3:00, and then the last group at 5:00 in the evening when only one more hour of daylight is left. Yet the boss gives *all* of the workers a full day's wage.

Understandably, the morning laborers complain that it is unfair that the later workers received the same wage as they did thus setting up a kind of competition, not cooperation, between all of the workers. The competitive fire here is not fueled by scarcity necessarily; presumably the boss has enough money to pay more than each would normally be due. Instead the competition between the morning and afternoon laborers is based on perceived fairness. So the two parties are not locked in a race for money, but they are stacked up against each other in a kind of competition where a "fair wage" is the prize.

But the boss (or God as is metaphorically meant by Jesus) says to the complaining workers (or to all of us): "I choose to give to this last the same as I give to you. Am I not allowed to do what I choose with what belongs to me? Or are you envious because I am generous?" And after he finishes the parable, Jesus adds, "So the last will be first, and the first will be last" (Matthew 20:14–16). The competitive zeal between the workers is diffused immediately by the boss with this reversal of who the winners and losers *really* are. Though Jesus does not downplay competition by substituting cooperation in its place, he does remove an important weapon from the typical argument: the social nature of competition. Each worker gets what is a fair day's wage, and what another worker receives is basically no business of his. Hence, when the last are elevated to first place, it is God's decision alone and is not based on the amount or quality of work performed that determines who comes out on top, as the parable suggests.

The parable of the Prodigal Son (Luke 15:11–32) and the story of Mary and Martha (Luke 10:38–42) convey similar criticisms of competition between people attempting to please God. These biblical snippets demonstrate that competition can focus attention onto the fellow competitor (the older brother over the prodigal son and to a lesser extent, Martha over Mary) when attention should be on God alone. And finally, Jesus' refusal to compete with the Roman authorities or at least fight for his own life reflects this overall diminution of the role of competition, even in matters of grave importance.

At other times, though, Jesus seems to encourage a kind of competition while refusing to come right out and endorse it. As we

saw in our chapter on pilgrimage, Jesus has some surprising words for
his disciples:

> Everyone therefore who acknowledges me before others, I also
> will acknowledge before my Father in heaven; but whoever
> denies me before others, I also will deny before my Father in
> heaven. Do not think that I have come to bring peace to the
> earth; I have not come to bring peace, but a sword. For I have
> come to set a man against his father, and a daughter against her
> mother, and a daughter-in-law against her mother-in-law; and
> one's foes will be members of one's own household. Whoever
> loves father or mother more than me is not worthy of me; and
> whoever loves son or daughter more than me is not worthy of
> me.
>
> (Matthew 10:34–39)

While most Christians would acknowledge that no human being truly
competes with Jesus for allegiance, a kind of competition is set up
between Jesus and all others, including family members. Jesus must
"win" the hearts of his followers over some pretty stiff competition.
In fact, he uses the image of a sword to convey that following him
instead of one's father and mother could be violent.

On the issue of scarcity, it is reasonable to assume that the gift of
salvation is not scarce or that there are not a limited number of spots
in heaven (the doctrine of the Jehovah's Witnesses aside). Heaven is
not a hotel, in other words. However, Jesus, as found in the book of
Matthew, does not seem to proclaim a message of universal salvation.
God will separate out the figurative sheep from the goats and grant
salvation to the sheep alone. Nowhere does Jesus say that all can be
sheep—there are and will be goats. Even though this statement does
not necessarily mean that the benefits of heaven are essentially limited
in some way, the sheep and goats metaphor does draw a firm distinction
between two groups of people and some *will* lose out in the end.
Competition as portrayed in all of these New Testament examples,
seems to admit that there are, in fact, winners and losers, but exactly
what is the meaning and proper role of competition is left for us to
speculate.

Competition in Sports

Unlike competition in religion where we have to look closely to find it, competition is front and center in sports. Indeed, all sports could be feasibly reduced down to competition—sports just happens to express it in a unique and culturally powerful way. To understand the tight connection between sports and competition we must ask ourselves, what would sports be if competition between participants were taken away? Or if cooperation replaced competition in sports, what would this look like? Because tackling the opposing players hurts its chances to score, in the spirit of cooperation, a team's defense would be encouraged to let the other team score. The tennis player would need to serve an easy ball to her opponent so that it could be hit back with little difficulty. The offense and defense and the opponents on the tennis court would be cooperating with each other, helping each other, in a way—in another way, this kind of behavior helps no one. These are obviously ridiculous scenarios that would never work in sports. The opposing sides have the same goal: to win the game. But only one team or individual can win, so cooperation makes no sense here. There must be winners and losers in sports or else the entire enterprise crumbles.

We see some of the problems with removing competition from sports play out in reality from time to time. There is a growing trend in youth sports to minimize the "winners and losers" part of a game. It is based on the fear that fostering competition in young children will only prevent cooperative behavior later on in life or perhaps do damage to the losing child's psyche. Accordingly, the tactic of handing out a championship trophy to *all* kids participating at the end of a game or tournament is something that has become common in youth sports leagues. Thoughtful criticism of this burgeoning practice admits that teaching cooperation to children is certainly a good thing. However, in sports, because competing against the opposing team or player is *essential* to the playing of the game, the "no losers" strategy decouples sports from competition thus making it difficult to call this activity "sports" at all. And because there are winners and losers in life, we may wonder how the "no losers" principle may play out in detrimental ways for these kids.

An example from the world of adult sports is instructive as well. The 2002 MLB All-Star game ended in a 7–7 tie. No regular season game is allowed to end in a tie, but the All-Star game is an exhibition game, and this particular one went two extra innings. Instead of letting the game play out until one team pulled ahead, as happens in regular season games, the coaches along with the commissioner of baseball decided to end it at a tie. Having no winner or loser, even in an exhibition game, drew so much criticism from the media and public alike that one could only conclude that a tie is anathema in baseball as it is in many other sports. We could speculate that one reason that soccer has had trouble cracking the American market on the professional level (and one reason that professional hockey recently changed its rules) is that it allows ties.

Competition is so ingrained in sports that it does not even have to involve another competitor. The marathoner often competes against his or her best previous time or in a way, against an older version of him or herself. Golfers have handicap, a number of strokes subtracted from the final score, that evens the playing field when competing with other golfers. But the handicap also serves as an individual benchmark that is competed against internally in the effort to lower it each time a round is played.

It bears stating that there is room for cooperation in sports, but it is almost always in the service of competition. Players on the same team compete for a starting position in practice, but they must help each other out in order to be successful in a real game. Off the field, this delicate balance between competition and cooperation does not need to be struck in terms of the ownership of a team where one owner or a small group of investors run a team; the owners do what they want in order to succeed without necessarily having to consult or cooperate with the fans. However, in the case of the NFL's Green Bay Packers, fans (over 350,000 of them) own the team as distributed through over 5 million shares, and therefore decisions at the top of this hierarchy must take into account the wishes and interests of a multitude. This unique example also highlights the distinction between private and public ownership of teams—the Packers will never leave town as opposed to any other privately owned team whose owner may get the financial incentive to move the team elsewhere.

As we celebrate the fortieth anniversary of Title IX in collegiate athletics, it's worth recalling that part of the Equal Opportunity in Education Act of 1972 states: "no person in the Unites States shall, on the basis of sex, be excluded from participation in, be denied the benefits of, or be subjected to discrimination under any education program or activity receiving Federal financial assistance." There is an inherent competition among the sports on a single campus for attention and funding. This competition was deemed unfair in the early 1970s; men's sports received a much larger slice of the monetary pie than women's sports despite the fact that relative levels of excellence were equal. In fact, in some cases there was no funding at all for women's sports. The remedy prescribed by Title IX exhibits a non-zero sum competitive structure where both men's and women's programs benefit, thus illustrating that instead of hurting men's sports (because of mandatory equal sharing of funds), all programs increased their funding over time for most schools. Ironically, what seemed a competitive move that would pit one sex against the other (may the best "team" win), both sets of teams won.

Beyond the goal of all parties benefitting, the issue of fairness is, of course, at the heart of the debates concerning gender and race in sports. Tennis star Venus Williams wrote an impassioned op-ed piece in the *New York Times* in 2006 imploring the All England Lawn Tennis Club that hosts Wimbledon each summer to pay equal prize money to men and women. She cited several compelling reasons in support of her point as she used the principle of competition as part of her argument. She wrote:

> Tennis is unique in the world of professional sports. No other sport has men and women competing for a grand slam championship on the same stage, at the same time. So in the eyes of the general public the men's and women's games have the same value.

(Williams 2006)

Paying women and men the same amount is the right thing to do in professional tennis because they compete on the same stage as well as generate similar amounts of money for the tournament. There is not a separate, smaller court for women or a different set of tennis balls used. That the top men's player would beat the top women's player is irrelevant here—the playing field in which each competes is even as their market values, hence the prize money, should reflect this reality.

The "Rooney Rule" in the NFL is similar. Black coaches, despite the overwhelming number of black players in the league, have historically been absent from the head coaching ranks for reasons that should not need elaboration. In the interest of fairness, the Rooney Rule forces teams to interview at least one racial minority candidate in their search for a new coach, which, as has been evidenced by two black coaches winning the Super Bowl in the 2000s, seems to have been a wise move for teams to make whether the rule was in place or not.

Simply because competition is indispensable in sports, this doesn't mean that it cannot yield less desirable results at times. All sports have rules that players must obey, and competition is bound by the rules in place. But at the highest level of sports, all athletes are stiff competition for each other. Therefore, finding an edge over an opponent is an understandable desire. Yet the drive to gain this competitive edge often pushes athletes to skirt the rules, if not to outright violate them. Surreptitiously holding on to the opponent's jersey to prevent him from jumping on a corner kick in soccer, trash talking into the ear of someone about to shoot a free throw, stealing signs from the catcher and communicating them to the batter on your own team—all of these actions bend or even break a rule. Yet they occur all of the time and are usually respected by fans and overlooked by referees.

Sometimes, the need to get a leg up on one's opponent encourages actions that cross a more important line when they break a rule or even a law. Out-and-out cheating to give one's team an edge was on full display when the NFL's New England Patriots were caught secretly filming the opposing team's pre-game practice, labeled "Spygate" by the media. Sammy Sosa illegally used a baseball bat filled with super ball shavings or a "corked bat" that helped the ball to go farther in 2003. Countless universities have been caught paying their athletes money or turning a blind eye to the gift-giving of rich alumni to entice recruits to attend their school. And most recently, the New Orleans Saints football team had a system of bounty payments doled out to players who injured opposing players during the 2010 and 2011 seasons. These rule violations warrant a more severe punishment than that of the mere bending of the rules on the field.

On an individual level, the use of performance-enhancing drugs is the primary way athletes obtain an illicit advantage. Hard work plus talent alone are expected to result in success or at least that is the expectation that most of us hold. When an athlete uses steroids, human growth hormone, hyper-oxygenated blood, or even masking drugs to hide other drugs while others don't, the issue of fair play is raised and sentences are often handed down. Lance Armstrong, seven-time winner of the Tour de France, was stripped of all of his titles because of doping allegations that were finally confirmed by former teammates. Similarly, Marion Jones, American track and field star, was forced to surrender her five medals from the 2000 Olympic Games after testing positive for erythropoietin, a hormone that increases the production of red blood cells. And the conclusion that eighty Major League Baseball players were linked to performance-enhancing drugs in the late 1990s and early 2000s made this the biggest drug scandal in sports history. The idea of fair play or an even playing field assumes first and foremost that all athletes are using natural means (talent and hard work primarily) to better their performance. An added, though perhaps unnatural, procedure that is acceptable nowadays is Lasik surgery that sharpens vision. But apparently taking steroids, a protein naturally found in the body, is not.

Leaving aside the question of what counts as natural and artificial and how the difference makes a difference to the fairness of the playing field, we still need to ask several questions as it relates to competition. Are these the actions of rogue players who willingly risk their careers and jail time as any common criminal would? Or is it simply the pressure to outperform the opposition that converts normally moral athletes into cheaters and liars? Or is the taking of *anything* that boosts performance immoral? And finally, is there something about competition itself, especially in sports (though we see it in business and politics too), that makes "winning at all costs" normalized and acceptable, no matter the questionable tactics employed to win?

While it is impossible to extract competition from sports, it is also near impossible to separate cheating in sports from the fierce drive to compete and win. Perhaps it is the excesses that stem from competition that religion and its ethics seek to curb. Some, after hearing of duplicitous athletes, may be reminded of their New Testament and be tempted to ask, "For what will it profit them if they gain the whole world but forfeit their life?" (Matthew 16:26). Or it is possible that competition and the need to win is so deeply embedded in sports that winning at any cost will never mean the forfeiting of a life for the dedicated athlete. That is, if sports is life and the cheating is never discovered.

Competition and Religion Today

We explained earlier that the tension between science and religion rendered religious institutions less powerful than scientific ones under the tenets of secularization theory, to say nothing of our current postsecular age. Put differently, science won the competition with religion for much of the last 300 years. But as Rodney Stark and William Sims Bainbridge eloquently argue, this is not the proper way to understand the narrative of secularization. Instead of interpreting the rise of science as a sign that scientific thinking is inherently better than religious thinking, we should think of both competing in the market-place of ideas, though not necessarily the *same* marketplace. In some enclaves of a society, science and religion do compete in the same marketplace, but in others, religion is really operating in its own market-place. When the secular and sacred are thought of in this way, instead of always assuming that science and religion are competing for the same prize, they often compete within their own respective domain leaving both relatively intact while elevating the role of competition in each discourse.

The more appropriate way to think about the progress of science and its secularizing influence, according to Stark and Bainbridge, is as such:

> Sometimes the pace of secularization speeds or slows, but the dominant religious organizations in any society are always

becoming progressively more worldly, which is to say, more secularized. The result of this trend has never been the end of religion, but merely a shift in fortunes among religions as faiths that have become too worldly are supplanted by more vigorous and less worldly religions.

(Stark and Bainbridge 1985, 2)

Looking sociologically at what they call "religious economies," they argue that the religious marketplace is characterized by the competitive offers of opportunities that pit the religions that become too worldly (those accommodating modern culture) against the "innovative" or "revival" new religious movements that assert the supernatural component of religion in novel ways. Indeed, "religions are social enterprises whose primary purpose is to create, maintain, and exchange supernaturally based general compensators" (Ibid., 172). And "new religions constantly appear in societies" that reassert the existence and power of the supernatural to provide a very unique compensator—salvation. The fervor and engagement of these latter new religious movements capture a market share from the religious traditions that soften the role of the supernatural so that overall religious participation remains intact regardless of the authority of science (Ibid., 3).

The reason that the presence of the supernatural in a religion has been a time-tested mark of success is that the believed reward for obeying supernatural dictates is an other-worldly salvation—a reward that cannot be provided by other producers in the market. As that which satisfies the human search for deep existential answers, religion behaves no differently from corporations or sports teams: All take advantage of the weaknesses of competitors and constantly strive to improve their game to win more converts/consumers. The "entrepreneur model of cult innovation" ("cult" is a pejorative term that was meant to be merely descriptive for the authors. "New Religious Movements" is preferred today) put forth by Stark and Bainbridge includes ten ideas:

1. Cults are businesses that provide product for their customers and receive payment in return.
2. Cults are mainly in the business of selling novel compensators, or at least freshly packaged compensators that appear new.

3. Therefore, a supply of novel compensators must be manufactured.
4. Both manufacture and sales are accomplished by entrepreneurs.
5. These entrepreneurs, like those in other businesses, are motivated by the desire for profit, which they can gain by exchanging compensators for rewards.
6. Motivation to enter the cult business is stimulated by the perception that such business can be profitable, an impression likely to be acquired through prior involvement with a successful cult.
7. Successful entrepreneurs require skills and experience, which are most easily gained through a prior career as the employee of an earlier successful cult.
8. The manufacturer of salable new compensators (or compensator packages) is most easily accomplished by assembling components of pre-existing compensator systems into new configurations or by further developing successful compensator systems.
9. Therefore, cults tend to cluster in lineages. They are linked by individual entrepreneurs who begin their careers in one cult and then leave to found their own. They bear strong "family resemblances" because they share many cultural features.
10. Ideas for completely new compensators can come from any cultural source or personal experience whatsoever, but the skillful entrepreneur experiments carefully in the development of new products and incorporates them permanently in his cult only if the market response is favorable.

(1985, 178–179)

Reading these ideas about the emergence of new cults that become new religions, one gets the impression that this could very well be a manual of how to start a new business. Treating beliefs as if they were marketable commodities allows Stark and Bainbridge not only to appreciate the cultural relevance of the religious industry among others but also to help us understand the persistence of religion today in a capitalistic market where *all* items are potential commodities.

The American scene has historically been a particularly good "fertile ground for new religions" such as Mormonism, Cult Communes, churches of New Thought, Theosophy and Spiritualism, Occult

Orders, Wiccans, Satanists, Pagans, and what they label "Jesus People" (Ibid., 189). These general headings of American-born religious movements are all derivations from older, traditional religions but with a new twist or ritual, a new set of beliefs, or a different supernatural order that is responsive to the needs of a community. The Mormon Church, with its original 70,000 settlers in Utah, now numbers over 14 million worldwide—just as numerous as the Jews who have been around for 5,000 years. No longer a fringe group, Mormons see themselves as a global force to be reckoned with. A more recent example is the Church of Scientology, created by L. Ron Hubbard in 1952 as an outgrowth of his earlier self-help system called "Dianetics", which is now estimated to have 8 million followers. Less known is Nuwaubianism, an umbrella term used to refer to the doctrines and teachings of the followers of Dwight York that originated as a Black Muslim group in New York in the 1970s. One cannot predict what market share Newaubianism will command in the future or what competitive edge they might have, but as long as they provide enticing compensators, they certainly have a shot.

Understanding contemporary religions as competitors in an economic-like market is a novel way of thinking about the role religion plays in our culture. Perhaps this makes sense in the American landscape where consumer culture, as we have mentioned before, has taken over so many facets of our existence. And this reality even drives devout and committed believers whose religion may discourage competition with people of other faiths or with people within their own faith tradition. In this game, there are winners, so to speak—those churches whose numbers are on the rise—and losers—those who must close their doors because of a lack of members.

The precarious position of the Jews as God's "chosen people"—a double-edged sword that signals primacy by decree and its attendant responsibility to the divine—is not a position shared by most in the rest of the religious world where the number of members signals not only financial success but an exclusive procurement of the truth. Cornering more of a market share, then, can be defended theologically (more people are "being saved") even when business-like marketing efforts constitute the tactics for increasing the number of saved souls.

While many decry a church's focus on the size of its religious community and its blatant use of marketing strategies to build membership, given the infiltration of market ideology into the American mindset, it should not surprise us that theologies are fashioned to justify these practices. Yet, instead of lamenting this state of affairs, it would be prudent to remember Stark and Bainbridge's work that finds that religions have been competing with each other for converts for thousands of years.

Competition in Religion and Sports

Despite Stark and Bainbridge's insistence that religion is separate from other "secular" industries and therefore not always in direct competition with them, American religion has no choice but to be immersed in our capitalist consumer culture. It is in this cultural context or on a fiber of this cultural web where religion often meets sports. Whether religion and sports perceive themselves as sister or complementary "industries" whose offerings please Americans in equal, however different, measures, they remain attractive options for the rich and poor alike. And it is in this sense that they often are mistaken as replacements for one another, as if one cannot choose both in the same purchase. The reality of the matter is that you can go to church *and* watch the game without having to make the false choice of preferring the one over the other or without doing damage to one by paying attention to the other. It is their participation in the same consumer culture that permits such a possibility.

The *internal* competition in these respective industries and the apparent *external* competition between these two industries seem to have no effect on their respective growth—both are fervently engaged in by a mass audience. What makes a comparison between religion and sports fascinating in terms of competition is that while sports is wholly committed to competition, religion is presumed to eschew it. Let competition thrive in the sports world, we seem to say, and keep religion outside of this vortex of hustle and bustle with all the ugliness that can accompany it. We'd like to believe that religion can be the sanctuary of pristine holiness where competitive instincts are overcome by a cooperative spirit that includes generosity and charity, communal giving, and spiritual yearning. This portrayal, though, is neither real nor even wholly ideal. It's not real because competitive market forces permeate faith institutions, whether they attempt to resist the forces or not. And it may not be ideal because, as Stark and Bainbridge point out, competition among religious traditions usually rewards those that push what makes religion unique instead of commonplace.

This is not to say that everything religious and everything having to do with sports revolves around numbers alone. Nor is this a way of reducing the religious meaning or the spirit of sportsmanship to commodities that are bought and sold in the marketplaces of our society. Instead, admitting that competition infects both sports and religion stands as a recognition that 24/7 marketing strategies are indeed gunning for everyone's attention *and* for everyone's soul. Moreover, contemporary culture has become linguistically and visually more homogenized as the same media technologies are used for wildly varying types of discourse. Sermons are now broadcast on television and on live internet streams, just as sports games are. Millions watch the selection of the new Pope in Rome with baited breath the way many watch the NFL draft. And the arrest of a famous athlete occupies the same spot on the nightly news as the arrest of a well-known pastor.

As much as we try to separate the spiritual from the mundane, our religious devotion from our love of competitive sports, these two industries or economies end up lodged in the same space and are forced to utilize similar means to survive. We bump into one while looking for the other. And what heightens this situation is the fact that both industries display some form of internal competition within themselves. A boundary between the *appearance* of religion and sports is truly blurred, and their *actual* authentic practices are more easily confused, despite declarations to the contrary.

When ancient gladiators offered momentary entertainment and priests promised eternal salvation, the stadium and the Temple were never mistaken for each other, lest we forget Jesus' overturning of the money changers' tables. Now that both places are equally accessible through television and laptop screens, the sacredness of the one doesn't stand out nearly as much in contrast to the worldliness of the other.

A push of a button on a remote control or a click of a mouse can transfer the viewer from one to the other with incredible ease and very little thought. When the movement between religion and sports can happen so seamlessly and the tactics used to compete for our attention are largely the same between the two, then it becomes more difficult for religion to claim superiority over sports and vice versa.

6
WORK

In physics, work is the simple expenditure of energy. In fact, energy is defined as the ability to do work. So anytime energy is expended, we are doing work in this sense. In a more specific sense, work is what we do for a living. We work or we use energy at a job in order to make money that supports our lives. Making money may not be the most important reason that we work; we may work to better society, to raise children, or even to please God with a certain kind of job or with the way that we work, no matter the job. It is this specific meaning of work that defines it as that which we do for a living, whether the job produces a paycheck or not (raising a family at home, for instance), that holds great significance for humanity. Every member of a society has a relationship to work.

True, work does not necessarily determine our entire lives or give us ultimate meaning. There are those who find that activities in their leisure time are far more satisfactory and meaningful than their 9-to-5 job. Then there are those who do not work at all because they are either reluctantly or gleefully unemployed or because they inherited enough from their family. And there are those who constantly seek to avoid sustained work by engaging in quick get-rich schemes or by buying lottery tickets daily. With the varying ways to relate to work, it should be clear that it is almost completely unavoidable (whether one works or not) and hence has had a major bearing on our worldview (religious or not).

The tie between work and religion is one that we may struggle to make when thinking about either. This is so because of the dividing line separating the Monday through Friday work week and the weekend in which we presumably take a break and/or reserve Friday night/Saturday or Sunday for worship and a rest from work, depending on the religion. However, Americans are increasingly having trouble doing just that. They work longer hours than workers in most other developed countries, and the typical American middle-income family puts in an average of eleven more hours a week in 2006 than it did in 1979. The reasons for this trend are usually cast in economic and political terms, but they also have cultural sources. Despite the desire by most to work fewer hours for the same or comparable pay, it is a strong work ethic that is embedded in the American psyche that can override the pursuit of such a working life. But where does this work ethic come from? And why is it not as pronounced in some other countries? And finally, what is the role of work and its ethic in religion, sports, and the relationship between the two?

Work in the Bible

The very first account of human beings in the Bible has to do with work. And because the Adam and Eve story is still a powerful myth for many, the way that work is dealt with by God in the story has an influence on the way work is viewed today. As recounted earlier in our book, before the Fall, Adam and Eve lived in perfect harmony with God and the surrounding creation. Perfection seemed to entail the absence of work, at least in one version of the story. One author's rendition of the creation story (there was more than one author of the creation story found in Genesis) has Adam receiving food without having to farm the land for it. "God said, 'See, I have given you every plant yielding seed that is upon the face of all the earth, and every tree with seed in its fruit, you shall have them for food.'" (Genesis 1:29). Another version has Adam tilling and keeping the Garden of Eden, yet he is allowed to eat of the trees with one exception, of course.

Adam and Eve do eat of the forbidden tree, and their relationship to work changes drastically afterwards. God decrees the punishment to Eve, "I will greatly increase your pangs in childbearing; in pain you shall bring forth children," and to Adam, "cursed is the ground because of you; in toil you shall eat of it all the days of your life . . . By the sweat of your face you shall eat bread . . ." (Genesis 3:17, 19). No longer will food be provided for free; Adam must work the land with sweat and toil in order to eat. In this way, work (that which we now take for granted as a necessary activity) is contrasted with an ideal state of abundance. As the soil is cursed, the work needed to extract food from it will now involve toil and sweat. And as the common Christian interpretation of "the Fall" goes, all future generations must pay for the sins of Adam and Eve by working, too. In addition to work-as-punishment, it is also now a divine command. This allows for the *possibility* that work is also good, as it is decreed by God, despite its original association with human disobedience.

This dynamic of work-as-punishment and leisure-as-reward runs throughout the Bible. The Israelites as slaves in Egypt are working in a hostile environment. Here, work is a type of punishment within the context of slavery. Important, though, is the way the Promised Land is described upon their release from captivity but before they actually reach it. It is a land of "milk and honey" in which food and water are readily available and inexhaustible:

> [A land] with flowing streams, with springs and underground waters welling up in valleys and hills, a land of wheat and barley, of vines and fig trees and pomegranates, a land of olive trees and honey, a land where you may eat bread without scarcity, where you will lack nothing . . .
>
> (Deuteronomy 8:7–9)

The image of ready-made food (no need to put your plow to the soil) and water springing up (no need to dig a well) stands in stark contrast to the grueling work performed as slaves in Egypt. Of course the Israelites did have to work eventually in Canaan, yet this work was part and parcel of their covenant with God as stewards of the land promised to Abraham.

In the book of Proverbs, we see work cast in a different light. The value of work is honored because it is deemed an essential part of human life. Moreover, more direction is given on how to do work properly as well as the kind of work that is godly. "In all toil there is profit, but mere talk leads to poverty" (Proverbs 14:23) Work is not contrasted with leisure where all is provided but with inaction. "One who is slack in work is close kin to a vandal" (Proverbs 18:9). It is not enough simply to work, one must work hard otherwise the worker is essentially stealing from his employer. "Do you see those who are skillful in their work? They will serve kings; they will not serve common people" (Proverbs 22:29). It is also important to be good at what one does at work. With the book of Proverbs, a different way of looking at work is presented. Work is a crucial facet of a human life that builds character and instills morality while helping to turn a profit. Work is not only something one does to repay God; it seems to have value in and of itself.

Inasmuch as work has been associated with and relegated to each individual, there is also a sense of a communal contribution through work that we find in scripture. We can see this in the sending out of Jacob's twelve sons to start their own tribe, which later become the Twelve Tribes of Israel (see Genesis 49:1–28). Each son has his special gifts and aptitudes that eventually are understood as duties to his tribal family. When the twelve tribes function together as the larger Israeli society, the society runs more smoothly than if each tribe was working for itself alone. This is not exactly what we eventually refer to as division of labor in advanced economies, but it comes close enough to suggest that when every member of society works with the good of the community in mind, the whole of society benefits. This is also not quite collaboration in terms of this person helping that person accomplish a task, but rather it bespeaks of an efficiency that takes advantage of one's specialization for the general good of the group. It is similar to what we suggested in the previous chapter about competition and collaboration, where the one can work in conjunction with the other to the advantage of all involved.

Work continues to be thought of primarily as a character-building enterprise rather than a punishment as we move into the New Testament. We see a subtle tribute being paid to certain kinds of jobs in Christian scripture. Jesus was a carpenter, his disciples were primarily fishermen, and Paul was a tentmaker. It seems that rich men, tax collectors, money changers, and high priests are not as respected by Jesus as are his own disciples. What are we to make of this distinction as it regards work? Perhaps Jesus sought out disciples from the artisan class and challenged those who worked in professions that did not produce anything material because of his own experience of being a carpenter. Or perhaps he held that the manual labor that produces fish, tables, or even tents is a more honest, character-building activity than merely handling money. Though the scriptures are not explicit, the occupations of the disciples and the rebuking of those in certain professions can lead us to a conclusion such as this. Alternatively, one may believe that God cares little about *what* one does for a living but rather *how* one does it—with honesty, brotherly love, and dignity.

So where does a strong work ethic enter the picture in the biblical narrative? There are verses in Proverbs that speak highly of hard work, but this kind of admonition is largely absent in the New Testament as conveyed, to a degree, in the parable of the laborers in the vineyard. In fact, the Bible is not considered a primary source for the work ethic displayed in the citizenry throughout American history. It traces its origins not to the Bible or to the early Christian Church but, according to Max Weber, to John Calvin writing in sixteenth-century Europe.

One of Calvin's key doctrines, predestination, states that God chooses or predestines people for heaven before they are even born. This means, in theologically troubling fashion, that God doubly predestines those for hell, too. Calvin states:

> We call predestination God's eternal decree, by which he compacted with himself that he willed to become of each man. For all are not created in equal condition: rather, ethereal life is foreordained for some, eternal damnation for others. Therefore, as any man has been created to one or the other of these ends, we speak of him as predestined to life or to death.
>
> (Calvin 1960, 926)

The problem for humanity, even if you are in the "elect," as Calvin called this fortunate group, is that only God knows who is in and who is out. While arguing that certain internal knowledge of one's fate in the afterlife is impossible, Calvin claims that there are external signs that one can display that may signal possible inclusion in the elect. Showing that one is a good Christian through hard work becomes a primary means of revealing the probability that one is saved.

The way Calvin couched this idea was to ask, how could a member of the elect be lazy? God simply would not choose such a person to enjoy the afterlife in heaven. Therefore, Calvin demands that a strong work ethic be present in all work that one does to ensure that the outward sign of God's favor is visible. That said, working hard produces more wealth, therefore wealth was good for Calvin. However, money was to be saved or invested in ways that helped out the society, but not spent on oneself on luxuries or on ostentatious items—a *show* of wealth is most certainly *not* a sign of being in the elect according to Calvin for it represents greed, pride, and the desire to appear special in the world when the real treasure is in heaven. And, perhaps strangely, using profits to help others achieve wealth but not to help the poor was viewed by Calvin as downright sinful. Only through one's *own* labor can divine favor be bestowed.

Calvin's doctrine had the effect of raising the status of work and the ethic that animates it to new levels in the growing Protestant Christian community—a status still in place in America today. Even though the biblical text may lack this kind of feverish language about work, Calvin transforms the way work is approached through a novel interpretation of God's relationship to creation—so much so that this connection between God's will and the work ethic has worked its way into the modern lexicon. "Idle hands are the devil's tools" and "God helps those who help themselves" are just two examples of common phrases that demonstrate the tight relationship that religion has with a certain way of approaching work, despite the absence of such phrases in the Bible.

Work in Sports

If work, at its most basic level, is the expenditure of energy, then an incredible amount of work gets done on a daily basis in the sports world. From practice to training to the effort put in during the event itself and then back to the weight room after the game, athletes can never completely avoid working and working hard at that. The talent that one is born with is akin to the gift of abundance in the Garden of Eden—without work, gifts will be squandered, talent will atrophy, and winning will never come. Or as basketball legend Larry Bird has said, "A winner is someone who recognizes his God-given talents, works his tail off to develop them into skills, and uses these skills to accomplish his goals." If receiving God-given talent is aristocratic, working hard is democratic—it is equally available to all. As New York Yankee Derek Jeter wisely quipped, "There may be people that have more talent than you, but there's no excuse for anyone to work harder than you do." Indeed, sports furnishes us with, perhaps, the clearest lens through which to see what work is and to understand what it means in twenty-first century America.

While becoming a successful athlete always entails working diligently at one's craft, professional athletes are paid for their work, just as all working people are. Most professional leagues, in fact, pay handsomely for the athlete's services, while many minor league or semi-pro leagues pay a bare minimum salary. In the top men's professional leagues, the minimum salary dwarfs most other entry level salaries, including those in the women's professional leagues. The *minimum* salary in the NFL in 2012 was $390,000, $473,000 in the NBA, $525,000 in the NHL, and $480,000 in MLB. The maximum salary a player can earn in each of these leagues has no real ceiling, though mandated salary caps for an entire team often keep individual salaries at a lower level than they would be on the open market.

For perspective, Alex Rodriguez of the New York Yankees makes $30 million each year, and Kobe Bryant of the Los Angeles Lakers pulls in $25 million per season. It is these kinds of extravagant, almost incomprehensible numbers that often have casual fans shaking their heads. When a season only lasts six months at the most and these athletes get star treatment everywhere they go, is this fair compensation for the actual work they do? Defenders of their salaries will often employ a market ideology by arguing that if fans were not willing to shell out money for tickets and watch games on TV, which generates advertising money, these salaries would not be possible. But apparently they are. Owners whose primary interest is making money on their team would not normally spend this kind of money if a return on their investment were not forthcoming.

And while some top level athletes rest on their laurels, most put in the hard work needed to succeed, thereby earning their salary. Contrary to the skeptical observer, pro athletes work year round through training camps that precede each season as well as in off-season personal workout sessions. Hence, a strong work ethic is needed to fuel the grueling workouts and long practices, especially after the season is over. However, not all athletes subscribe to a robust work ethic all of the time in order to achieve success. And it is here that sports shines a particularly bright light on the relationship between American culture and the Protestant work ethic.

The use of performance-enhancing drugs (PEDs) is a classic circumvention of the hard work that is usually assumed to separate good athletes from great ones. Recall from the chapters on pilgrimage and competition that an even playing field among athletes is presupposed by fans. Hence a work ethic is *the* distinguishing value possessed by successful athletes, all other things being equal. When a player decides to inject him or herself with a drug, hormone, or hyper-oxygenated blood, a short cut is taken around time in the gym, and the work ethic is thus sidestepped and devalued. Though cutting corners occurs every day at work in the non-sports world (leaving early from work or spending less time than necessary to do the job well), when athletes are caught taking PEDs, something bigger is at stake.

As mentioned earlier, many PEDs are illegal, and therefore their ingestion is immediately put into a different category than checking the Internet at work. Yet it is the unwritten rule of the strong work ethic rather than illegality (because some prohibitions were in place until more recently), that plays a bigger role in the public's interpretation of the relationship between working hard and taking drugs. Because PEDs build muscle mass in conjunction with working out, getting stronger requires less work than for the athlete who only works out. Hence the work ethic is skirted to a large degree with even better results in the end than there would be in their absence. The case of steroids in MLB illustrates this very well, and the varying ways that fans and the media reacted to certain players who were accused of using steroids in the early 2000s reveal that the value of the work ethic still resonates loudly in American culture.

Mark McGwire shattered the 37-year-old single season home run record in 1998 only to be bested by Barry Bonds a mere three years later. In 1998, there was not a steroid cloud hanging over the head of McGwire, a white player, as he was progressing towards the record. In fact, he was named *Time Magazine*'s "Hero of the Year." By 2001, however, Barry Bonds, an African-American, could not hit a home run during his historic season without the steroid question being raised. McGwire went largely unscathed by the media and fans alike for years, until 2005 when he testified before Congress and denied that he ever took steroids. Both players hit 70 home runs, and both players looked immensely bigger than before when breaking their respective records. Yet Bonds has received far more criticism than McGwire, which continues to the present day.

Why is this so, and what does it have to do with the relationship between sports and work? It is true that Bonds was less congenial with fans and the media than McGwire and that McGwire admitted in 2010 to taking steroids—something that Bonds has never done even though he was found guilty of obstructing justice in this matter in 2011. Beyond these differences, it is possible that race also plays a role in the differing treatments. A lingering stereotype of African-Americans is that they are lazy. The racially tinged images of the "Welfare Queen" and the black man who will do anything to avoid work are damaging, untrue portrayals but are ones that continue to circulate in American culture. In this light, the suspicion that Bonds took steroids to get around putting in the hard work is bolstered by the stereotype, whereas many Americans had trouble classifying McGwire as lazy or as someone who would deliberately shun the honest work needed to be successful.

Race is certainly not the only factor guiding public reaction, yet if it plays even a minor role here, we can see that the idea of the tough work ethic, when attached to enduring racial stereotypes, is alive and well. Sports discloses the value placed on the American work ethic, through the stories of PEDs in particular, because of its deep ties to working hard in general. The difference between the successful athlete and the one who loses is often so small that their respective commitments to a work ethic, even though we still can only speculate, may be the only criterion that we have at our disposal to judge true greatness. And it is a powerful criterion that we have the legacy of Calvin's theology to thank for, whether those judging Barry Bonds are aware of it or not.

Work and Religion Today

Unlike some of the terms we've discussed in previous chapters, religion does not seem to have an influence on the work ethic as seen in sports. Working hard, doing a job right, treating others ethically through work—all occur daily without the worker (or athlete) needing to make reference to religion. This would not surprise German sociologist Max Weber (1864–1920) in the least. Over one hundred years ago, Weber constructed a famous argument in his book, *The Protestant Ethic and the Spirit of Capitalism* (Weber 1958), that asserted that the theology of the Protestant Reformation was one of the primary causes for the success of capitalism in certain societies. It is actually *his* analysis of Calvin that popularized terms such as the Protestant work ethic, delayed gratification, and saving, not spending—all of which are well-integrated into the fabric of capitalism.

At the end of his book, Weber assesses the work ethic in his own day and age. He acknowledges that a strong work ethic is still present in most working people. However, its connection to religion, which Calvin made explicit, has been severed. A *vocation* or *calling* that used to connect God's will to one's work no longer is able to put the two together in any real sense. Some people may still believe that God has a plan for them and that it is God's will for all to work hard, but work and its ethic are now disconnected from any religious justification for it. He describes this reality in stark terms.

> The idea of duty in one's calling prowls about in our lives like the ghost of dead religious beliefs. Where the fulfillment of the calling cannot directly be related to the highest spiritual and cultural values, or when, on the other hand, it need not be felt simply as economic compulsion, the individual generally abandons the attempt to justify it at all.
>
> (Weber 1958, 182)

For Weber, work has become rationalized (its goal is to be merely efficient in order to produce the greatest number of commodities with the least energy) and bureaucratized (it is embedded within an organizational structure that, in an impersonal way, makes sure efficiency is occurring) in twentieth-century capitalistic economies. Rationalization and bureaucratization create an "iron cage" that traps work and does not allow the external God, who presumably calls people to a vocation, to infect our job. Religious language is still spoken inside the cage, but work itself cannot be informed directly by God who "sits on the outside."

If religious belief is merely a ghost that rattles around our working life but does not animate it anymore, what does this bode for the future of religion, work, and the relationship between the two? Weber's argument is predicated on the contention that our world is slowly becoming "disenchanted." What Weber means by this is that the old enchanted world, with its supernatural enlivened natural institutions (work *was* a call from God), has lost its standing. A split between the natural and supernatural has occurred, leaving certain institutions, such as education, the family, the State, and work, to run on their own without the need to justify themselves on religious morality or the Bible. The separation of Church and State in the U.S. and the elimination of religion from most science classrooms are but two of the consequences of a disenchanted world.

However, as we cited in the Introduction, in the hundred years since Weber wrote his influential book, while the world has most certainly been subject to disenchanting forces, religion has not gone the way of the dinosaur; nor have the work ethic, vocations, *and* capitalism. A return to an enchanted world is no longer possible with the establishment of the authority of science, so how does religion and work fit together today, if in fact they still can? Weber rightly connects a disenchanted world with a growing secularized one where the religious and secular (read capitalism) are separated by the bars on the cage. Hence, work and religion can team up again only if the door of the iron cage has been opened.

What has begun to open the cage doors and change the relationship between religion and work is the drastic change in the nature of work from Weber's day to our own in the twenty-first century. Machines have long since replaced the human corn picker, the cubicle now replaces the factory assembly line, and the computer replaces the door-to-door salesman. In this post-industrial, service-based economy of ours, work is now "softer" (no sweat on the brow) than it used to be. There are still manual jobs to be done in America, but immigrants, who have yet to go "soft," seem to be the ones most willing to perform them. Again, service-based jobs do not correspond to a slackening of the work ethic even though fewer and fewer hands are getting dirty. What then of the work ethic and religion in this new environment?

Contrary to Weber and what one may assume about the lessening role of religion in these contemporary examples, it is *still* difficult to completely detach religion from the work ethic that remains prevalent—the ghost still haunts. Instead of looking for Calvinist-styled vocations in modern America, it is more fruitful to view the relationship between religion and work through a postsecular lens. Again, the relationship between the religious and the secular under postsecularism is one of negotiation, not conflict; or in other words, the iron cage cannot keep capitalism and religion from flowing into one another. Hence Weber's work ethic and a religious vocation can be reunited, though under different conditions than before. And a service-based economy that now relies on the Internet to connect businesses to clients in different parts of the globe helps in breaking down boundaries of all kinds, including the ones that hold religion back from mixing with the secular.

A case in point: the fact that scholars now talk openly about *human* capital that can be invested in spiritual, humanitarian, or economic projects without contradiction is proof positive that capitalism and religion are not quite as segregated as they once were. "Spiritual economies"—placing value on one's faith, the way one puts value on a commodity—seem to parallel mundane economies, in which the marketplace rules all relationships (Rudnyckyj 2010). The "Faith at Work" movement is stronger than it has ever been insofar that it now openly pushes for the de-silencing of vocal expressions of faith within the workplace while grappling for ways for religion to express itself appropriately at work. Self-help books, such as Steven Covey's *The 8th Habit: From Effectiveness to Greatness*, use the language of a religious vocation even when speaking to a secular, business audience:

> Perhaps the most important vision of all is to develop a sense of self, a sense of your own destiny, a sense of your unique mission and role in life, as a sense of purpose and meaning. When testing your own personal vision first ask yourself: Does the vision tap into my voice, my energy, my unique talent? Does it give me a sense of "calling," a cause worthy of my commitment?
>
> (Covey 2004, 72)

Though Calvin's vocation may have to play to a more secular crowd in the twenty-first century, the idea of a religious vocation remains relevant in churches as well as corporations. And when looking at this through a postsecular prism, we should not be surprised.

Work in Religion and Sports

When people meet each other for the first time they are likely to ask, "what do you do," rather than, "who are you?" Asking about one's occupation is a revealing way to understand who you are dealing with without putting them off with more personal, deeper questions. The presumption is that you choose one of the most important facets of your life: your career. Hence, your work not only reveals what tasks you perform during the week but also may divulge who you are and what is important to you. For example, if you are a firefighter or a first-grade teacher, you are immediately associated with serving the community as opposed to the stockbroker on Wall Street who is perceived to only serve him or herself, whether these stereotypes are fair or not.

This way of using work as a window into who one is belies the Calvinist shift from work as such to the work ethic. For Calvin, the ultimate goal is to be in union with God in heaven. Work alone cannot get you there, but the ethic that informs work—the way you perform your duties—may at least display where you stand in cosmic terms. The ethic, then, is a set of principles about what one should and should not do, how to distinguish between right and wrong, good and evil. Just knowing what people do for a living tells you little about their principles. There are honest used car salesmen and selfish priests, to be sure.

As regards ethics, there is, though, the letter of the law and the spirit of the law. It is the fine line between the two that religious and athletic institutions as well as individuals sometimes quibble about or test. For example, many of the doping cases in professional cycling circles were dismissed because secondary effects from vitamins and other supplements, which are legal, may contain particles that have similar effects to steroids and other enhancing drugs. Were cyclists intent on circumventing the spirit of the law by complying with the letter of the law? Likewise, priests and pastors know that they cannot "sell" a preferred place in the afterlife, yet they zealously collect alms and funds from parishioners on a weekly basis and recognize donors through plaques on pews and benefactor lists in bulletins. While not quite heaven, something of permanence is returned for donations. In all of these situations, simply adhering to the stated rules of the game or to religious laws isn't sufficient for answering more subtle questions about proper behavior.

In addition to the complexity of interpreting and following laws associated with sports and religion, both the letter and the spirit, there is also the context within which such interpretations take place. In a culture defined primarily by dollars and cents, success is measured by results and not necessarily by the process of getting there, which often involves hard work and honesty. Luck can play a major role just as much as taking short cuts or even outright cheating (at times called white lies to minimize their immoral nature) does. Of course you have to be in the game to have a chance at winning, but how did you get there to begin with? Was it by chance that you stood out on that particular practice day when a scout came looking? Was it your daily dose of training that ensured you were picked up from a large lineup of equally qualified players? Was this choice made exclusively based on your skill or did your good looks contribute to it? Good genes are inherited, not earned, so what does this have to do with your work ethic as it relates to success? Similarly, some churches do better than others because their pastor is charismatic and/or physically attractive. Why should that matter?

Despite the periodic difficulty in connecting a work ethic with success or failure, we can still be certain that our outrage at athletes or religious leaders who take short cuts and fail to live up to our expectations testifies to the fact that we do connect morality to the work ethic. Hence, to this day the sense of whether someone is working hard or is a lazy freeloader is still the most profound weapon used to analyze situations that arise in both religion and sports. The work ethic illuminates such activities as lying and cheating as much as it does honesty and doing things the right way. While the work ethic has a more tenuous relationship with religion than it did in Calvin's day, contrary to Weber's assessment, a moral remnant is still associated with work.

Yet Weber is correct too: it is still challenging to justify hard work on the basis of what one believes is God's will, especially when many jobs in capitalistic societies are often mindless and less than satisfying. It is in this tension between the practical difficulty of drawing on religion to work hard and the persistence of the value of the work ethic that allows sports and religion to inform each other. There can be no question of the prominent place that the work ethic occupies in the successful athlete's regimen to the point that sports expresses one of, if not the clearest examples of people working as hard as any citizen. Yet, after the trophy is won, there may be a need to defend the amount of work and sacrifice endured that transcends winning alone. Was it all worth it? It could be the simple reassurance that the means to win was done the right way that eliminates the possibility of regret. And when morality is brought into the equation, religion is usually not close behind to help inform, reinforce, and even justify the decision to work extremely hard and never cut corners. It is here that the issue of work brings religion and sports together—each discourse supplying something that the other needs. Perhaps the reports of the death of the ghost of religious beliefs have been greatly exaggerated.

7

REDEMPTION

We have all heard the phrase, "everyone makes mistakes." It resonates today as it did in times past because it is true—no one is perfect, and no one likes to make mistakes either. We not only try to avoid making mistakes, but once we make one, especially one that negatively affects a fellow human being, our tendency is to make amends for the mistake made, which presumably helps us get beyond it. If these are truisms, then perhaps we can make two claims about human beings: we are frail and prone to failure, and we seek to minimize mistakes and then move past them as quickly as possible. Not all mistakes are created equal, though. Forgetting to brush your teeth is not as bad as forgetting to meet a friend for dinner or worse, forgetting a wedding anniversary. In other words, mistakes in etiquette (chewing with your mouth open) are glossed over more easily than moral mistakes (lying to your best friend), for good reasons.

A mistake, no matter its size, implies that something has been put out of place or that the orderly flow of life has been interrupted and upset. A husband remembering his wedding anniversary and acting accordingly is what should happen in the normal flow of a marriage; either forgetting the anniversary or even remembering it, but forgetting to buy a gift for his wife are mistakes that set the normal flow off course.

When a flow such as this is disrupted or improperly diverted, there is often a need to reestablish order so that life can run smoothly once again. Or when we make a mistake, relative to its gravity, we must rectify it somehow so that it does not continue to unsettle our lives and the lives of those around us.

Redemption is one of the terms that we use to describe the process of righting a wrong and restoring balance. If committing a mistake puts things out of place, the process of redemption or being redeemed puts them and our relationship to these things back in their rightful place. Redemption would not be necessary if we didn't have a propensity to make mistakes. And some mistakes are too troublesome to ignore, thus necessitating redemption.

Mistakes and the redemption that hopefully follows go hand-in-hand, yet in between a mistake and redemption often sits punishment. How can one be redeemed if the mistake against another has yet to be paid for in some way? But if punishment follows the mistake, the punishment needs to fit the crime. What is an appropriate punishment? Who decides? Also, who should grant redemption once the mistake is paid for? Can one redeem oneself or does the successful act of redeeming always need another to grant it? And if another is needed to redeem the one who made the mistake, what must be done? Is it earned or freely given? And finally, is it even possible to truly make amends for past wrongs or is redemption merely a soothing idea to our damaged and frail psyche? These questions complicate the movement from mistake to redemption, though both religion and sports have attempted to clarify the process.

Redemption in the Bible

It can be argued that the process of achieving redemption in society can trace its lineage back to religious articulations of the concept. Redemption is a crucial concept in the Bible because God's will and commandments are constantly being violated by humanity in the form of sin and as such, humanity is in dire need of redemption of the highest order. In fact, the opening story from the Bible tells of the first violation of divine will that stems from the exercising of free will.

Yet the Jewish concept of redemption and sin is less pronounced than that found in Christianity.

In the Hebrew Bible, several covenants are established and reaffirmed between God and the chosen people from Noah to Moses. To simplify to the extreme, one can argue that obedience to the Law was often ignored by the Israelites, such as their worshipping of the golden calf, and God punishes them swiftly and profoundly. Prophets step in to notify the Israelites of the nature of their sin against God, remind them of their covenantal obligations, and finally, state a prescription on how to get back in God's good graces. A passage from the prophet Jeremiah that explains why the Jews are in exile in Babylon and not in their Promised Land illustrates this well. In what follows, Jeremiah is speaking for God and, in rather strong figurative language, rebukes the Israelites for worshipping idols:

> If a man divorces his wife and she goes from him and becomes another man's wife, will he return to her? Would not such a land be greatly polluted? You have played the whore with many lovers; and would you return to me?
>
> (Jeremiah 3:1–2)

Yet later in the chapter, God gives them a way to make up for their sins:

> Return, faithless Israel, says the Lord. I will not look on you in anger, for I am merciful, I will not be angry forever. Only acknowledge your guilt, that you have rebelled against the Lord your God, and scattered your favors among strangers under every green tree, and have not obeyed my voice, says the Lord.
>
> (Jeremiah 3:12–13)

Here we see several steps laid out that delineate the process from sin to redemption for the Israelites. Recognition of the nature and gravity of their mistake and acknowledgment of responsibility for their sin provide the conditions under which it is possible for the Israelites to be redeemed. It is important to note that it is the *group* of Israelites and not a singular "you" that has "been with many lovers," and it is *all* of Israel that is "faithless" but can eventually "return."

Redemption is also the major theme of the most important Jewish holiday, Yom Kippur. Based on God's command to Moses to hold a "Day of Atonement" once a year, Yom Kippur is the day that all sins from the previous year will be forgiven by God if one repents and makes amends (Leviticus 26:23). However, this day only covers sins against God. Before Yom Kippur, Jews are to seek out all who they have wronged personally, ask for forgiveness, and hopefully receive it before being fully atoned for the year's sins. If the other person does not know that you are sorry and are seeking forgiveness, God will not clear the sin away. In this case, both God *and* the person who was wronged are able to offer redemption; only the one sinned against can grant redemption, though neither is obligated to do so.

In the New Testament, a different picture of both sin and redemption is painted. First of all, Paul and the fourth-century theologian, Augustine, interpret Adam and Eve's disobedience in the Garden of Eden as a cosmic event—one that potentially separates humanity from God permanently. In other words, if redemption is even possible for this sin, it will not come easy. This catastrophic breach in the relationship between God and humanity, according to many Christians, can only be bridged by a God/man, not by a fellow human being alone. The Fall is thought of by Paul as a debt that is owed God—Adam and Eve were given the keys to the kingdom, and they misused them. Only a "second Adam," Jesus Christ, who is believed to have redeemed the world with his self-sacrificial act on the cross, can sufficiently give God final satisfaction and make it right again. Paul's letter to the Romans sums up this idea:

> [W]e even boast in God through our Lord Jesus Christ, through whom we have now received reconciliation. Therefore, just as sin came into the world through one man, and death came through sin, and so death spread to all because all have sinned.
> (Romans 5:11–14)

By Jesus being fully human and fully divine (a doctrine established at the Council of Chalcedon, 451 C.E.), he alone is capable of taking on the sins of humanity *and* satisfying God once and for all for the debt incurred by Adam's grave error. The result is reconciliation with

God for those who believe that Jesus, in fact, accomplished this feat. And on this point, because many Christians consider that faith is all that is necessary to participate in Jesus' redemptive act, salvation is given by God to anyone who believes. Because sin is considered to be more cosmic in Christianity than in Judaism, redemption for Christians is an act that is to be performed by God alone through Jesus instead of in cooperation with humanity. Yes, one can sin against a neighbor and even against oneself, but these and other sins are the result of our fallen nature—a nature that only God, and not another human being, can restore. One cannot redeem oneself because all humans are flawed, sinful beings. Only a perfect, sinless being can redeem humanity, according to the Christian view of redemption.

Because the first sin is more situational rather than cosmic in Judaism (it's simply the first mistake, not the biggest one), redemption can occur on a more mundane level. In addition, the Jewish requirement for redemption is social, in that the community as a whole must undergo an annual process of redemption, especially insofar as individuals must ask forgiveness from each other. The Christian process of redemption, by contrast, is fully contained within Jesus' sacrifice on the cross, which can be accessed directly through an individual's faith.

We all know that making mistakes or committing sins, for the religious person, is an unavoidable fact of life. And we also know that mistakes do not sit well with us; amends need to be made and hopefully forgiveness or redemption is granted in the process. Within the biblical narrative, this process is not essentially different from the garden-variety apology that we make to those who we have harmed. However, when God is the one who has been harmed, the stakes are higher for the believer, and the steps taken to be redeemed often need to be drastic.

Redemption in Sports

In sports, as in religion, mistakes need to be rectified. But when an athlete's mistakes, whether on the field or not, are aired in front of millions of fans, the route to redemption differs greatly from the kind granted by God or another human being. To whom does the athlete go to seek redemption? Those he or she immediately hurt? The judge in court? Fans? The team owner? The league? The general public? God?

All or some of these? Or is Charles Barkley, NBA Hall of Famer, correct when he famously quipped in a commercial, "I am not a role model"? Does an athlete have any obligation to apologize for a mistake at all— is Barkley beholden to fans to make amends for acting badly or not? Unlike with religion, redemption of the public sports figure seems more complicated, but still desired.

With sports in general, there are mistakes made within a game demanding that amends be made. Penalty kicks in soccer, moving the football up 15 yards for an infraction, sitting in the penalty box in hockey—all are the result of breaking a rule with the punishment serving to pay back the other team. Yet it is difficult to say that redemption takes place for the penalized player in these cases. It may just be mere punishment to make up for the infraction, but the player is not necessarily "washed clean" by incurring the penalty. Nor is remorse required or forgiveness expected.

Sometimes, an entire sports career is in need of redemption. Usually, the marker of career success is a championship. For those athletes who were spectacular statistics-wise year after year, but were unable to win a championship in their sport, their "mistake" is not winning one and redemption can only come in the form of finally winning. Dan Marino, who retired from the NFL's Miami Dolphins in 1998 with the most passing yards in the league's history, still laments his lack of a Super Bowl ring 14 years later. "There's no doubt that that's the one thing [a championship] in my life and in sports, just feeling what that would be like. There's no doubt that there's sometimes I think about that, even today." Players, such as John Elway formerly of the Denver Broncos, and Dirk Nowitzki of the NBA's Dallas Mavericks, accomplished everything in their respective sports except a championship for their team. Both achieved this goal late in their careers, thus redeeming them in ways that great statistical seasons year in and year out could never accomplish.

Infractions and the need for redemption can also occur for athletes completely outside the game itself. These kinds of violations may entail the breaking of civil or criminal law, not just a rule of the game. For the normal citizen, breaking laws requires a penalty be paid, whether it be financial or jail time or even death. When a famous athlete breaks the law, however, he or she has to face not only the standard penalty as prescribed by the courts but also the judgment of fans, the team brass, and the league.

NFL quarterback Michael Vick was arrested in 2007 for helping to run an interstate dog fighting ring for which he served almost two years in prison. Upon release from prison, he expressed interest in playing football again. In a way, getting back on the field after jail time could serve to demonstrate that Vick had paid the price for his crime and was able to start again where he left off (as if nothing really happened). Football fans and animal lovers worldwide were unwilling to let him off the hook that easily. There were protests at his games and he received death threats when he began his career again for the Philadelphia Eagles. Apparently, for some, prison wasn't enough punishment for his crime. So, Vick appealed to the public by offering a seemingly sincere apology, volunteering at animal shelters, and vowing never to do anything like this again. And while these actions may have satisfied some, for other more offended observers, Vick will *never* be redeemed no matter the penance he pays. And for yet another group who still identifies him primarily as an athlete and not as a dog killer, redemption will arrive at the moment that he returns to form on the football field.

Golf extraordinaire, Tiger Woods, found himself in one of the biggest scandals in modern sports history. Winner of fourteen major championships, he was caught by several media outlets cheating on his wife with multiple women in November 2009. Granted, Tiger did not break the law or most certainly the rules of golf. And obviously, many athletes have been caught doing the very same thing and more have never been caught. But in Woods' case, he had managed to build up a reputation as a clean-cut family man. The public naïvely thought it knew something of his character and his behavior off of the course through television advertisements that presented him as such. Therefore, his repeated commission of adultery demanded that he go to a different set of authorities for redemption than Vick's, who was never thought of as a particularly upstanding man by fans.

Beyond asking forgiveness from his wife, who still divorced him a year later, Woods needed to restore his image both to his fans and his corporate sponsors. He did so in a nationally televised press conference in early 2010 where he said:

> I thought I could get away with whatever I wanted to. I felt that I had worked hard my entire life and deserved to enjoy all the temptations around me. I felt I was entitled. Thanks to money and fame, I didn't have to go far to find them. I was wrong. I was foolish.

We have in this statement all the markings of an *attempt* at gaining redemption: the explanation of why the mistake was made and then the acknowledgment of guilt. Woods also reported that he had checked into a sexual addiction rehab center for help and even invoked the religion he grew up with, Buddhism, as a means to convince the public that he needs something bigger than himself to change his ways. While satisfactory to some (at least he acknowledged his private failures publicly), others may have seen his *mea culpa* as a less-than-genuine attempt to curry favor with the fans who buy the products that he hocks. And as it was for Vick, redemption may not be complete for some fans until Woods regains the top spot in the golf world. Because playing great golf and becoming famous contributed to his fall in the first place, if his game never comes back, this could serve as a sign for some that he will always be paying for his transgression.

In the case of NBA superstar, LeBron James, the mistake, if one can call it that, was leaving his hometown team, the Cleveland Cavaliers, to join the Miami Heat in the summer of 2010. The city of Cleveland and the country at large bemoaned this act as one of treason—how dare he leave his successful small-market hometown team? Was there no loyalty to the fans who returned the loyalty on a nightly basis? James broke no law nor any rule of the game, but it was taken as a big thumb in the eye of an entire city. Perhaps it was a wise professional and financial move, but that alone has no redemptive quality in the case of James. In fact, he felt no need to apologize for the exodus and was actually surprised by Cleveland and the nation's reaction. In his case, redemption, if any was necessary, could *only* take place on the basketball court on which a championship, as he won in

2012 and 2013, would prove to everyone that his decision was justified and not a mistake at all. Possibly redeemed in the eyes of the basketball fan, Cleveland, though, continues to withhold its redemption of LeBron James, perhaps in perpetuity.

Another authority that athletes must, at times, ask for forgiveness from is the group of voters allowing or denying entrance into Halls of Fame. When a stellar playing career is over, one final confirmation that past mistakes are pardoned and a career is redeemed is needed by many athletes who qualify. Those who vote players into Halls of Fame, perhaps curiously, sometimes weigh the moral and legal transgressions committed by the athlete in their decision. As a result, potential entrants may decide to plead their case in public (as if it were to God) as an appeal to the voting body. If one made mistakes off the field during a career but those mistakes didn't affect the player's performance or stifle success, forgiveness may come quick. Michael Jordan and his overlooked gambling habit come to mind. On the other hand, Pete Rose, who spent twenty-three seasons as a player and five as a manager holds the all-time league record for hits (a record that will likely never be broken), yet has not received the same treatment. In 1989, Rose was accused of gambling on baseball games that he was managing. This, even more than steroid use, is perhaps the most despicable crime in sports—deliberately altering the outcome of a game to win an outside bet. Consequently, Rose was permanently banned from entering the Hall of Fame, which he, no doubt, would have entered absent these charges.

Redemption for Rose almost exclusively comes down to getting into the Hall of Fame. He must first appeal to the commissioner of baseball to lift the ban and then to the voters to let him in. If this happens, his career, his status as a great baseball player, and, as he has admitted, his status as a human being will be redeemed. Yet Rose has certainly not helped his case over the years and at times has seemed utterly disinterested in atoning for his past mistakes.

> I'm sure that I'm supposed to act all sorry or sad or guilty now that I've accepted that I've done something wrong. But you see, I'm just not built that way . . . So let's leave it like this: I'm sorry

it happened and I'm sorry for all the people, fans and family that it hurt. Let's move on.

(Curry 2004)

Though, years later, we see some level of admission of guilt and the desperate need for the redemption that commissioner Bud Selig can offer:

I felt the load was taken off my shoulders 14 months ago when I was able to tell Bud Selig the same thing that's in the book. To be honest with you, when I left Bud's office that day, I had a real good feeling. I personally thought I was going to be reinstated.

(Kindred 2011)

He has yet to be reinstated, and just like suspected steroid users Barry Bonds, Mark McGwire, and Roger Clemens, to name a few, Rose's mistake may simply be too grand for voters to overlook, despite his gaudy statistics.

How are we to think of the sin/redemption relationship in the cases we just described? The circuit of sin, acknowledgement of guilt, appeal to proper authorities, and finally redemption, is firmly in place in the sports world as it is in religion. The unique aspect of redemption in sports, though, is not only the variety of people that one can wound but also the multitude of authorities that must be consulted and appeased before redemption can occur. It may be unclear who has been offended by an athlete's mistake, who to go to for redemption, how redemption is granted, and finally whether redemption is even necessary when an athlete messes up. They are athletes with unique relationships with fans, but who's to say that Charles Barkley isn't right? Maybe the need for redemption presupposes that athletes have a responsibility to be upstanding citizens, but why should they? Given this distinctive relationship between mistakes and the redemption of the one who made the mistake in sports, the simple movement from mistake to redemption is far more complex than meets the eye.

Redemption and Religion Today

Despite the seeming clear progression from sin to redemption as presented in an individual biblical story, when applied in the world, the relationship between sin and redemption has become more complex as time has gone by. Perhaps the complexity is due to differing interpretations of sin and redemption given in the Hebrew Bible and then later in the New Testament. As noted earlier, the concept of sin has always been and still remains quite murky within Judaism despite the rituals performed during Yom Kippur. If, according to this view, the Fall constituted the first mistake committed by the first humans, then there is no converting a simple mistake into a sin against God for all time. How does this "first mistake" relate to future ones or should it?

With the introduction of a doctrine of Original Sin by Augustine in the fourth century C.E., Christians may have resolved this perceived problem to some extent, but they, likewise, haven't settled once and for all what counts as a sin. As Martin Luther knew all too well in the sixteenth century, one could just as easily commit a sin unknowingly as one could feel pious for performing a good act. Guilt is such a powerful feeling for many because it incorporates the recognition that one might have done something wrong in thought *and* deed. A guilty conscience is fed by both, and God can purportedly see through the veils of pretense and deceit projected by you. Worse, it is often difficult to gather the true motives that guide one's own conduct, and only a trusted friend or loved one can convey to you what you yourself deny out of blindness, self-protection, and self-delusion. This latter situation may call to mind the works of the Austrian psychologist, Sigmund Freud (1856–1939), who focused on our subconscious as the repository of true feelings that we have suppressed over time because of fear and the need to overcome it.

The notion of punishment is similarly not clear-cut. While the Jewish Law famously states the "an eye for an eye" principle of justice (Leviticus 24:20), the New Testament implores, "If someone strikes you on the right cheek, turn to him the other also" (Matthew 5:39). The only way to respond to aggression is not with judgment and violence, but with mercy and tolerance in the latter case. Punishment, then, becomes more difficult to discern than that given by a simple *quid pro quo* (something for something). This is especially true in the case of sins against God where a direct, straightforward relationship is more difficult to establish and a transgression cannot be simply paid for by sacrificing an animal on an altar anymore. Moreover, how does one punish a sinful thought that violates God's will? How can a limited human punishment, if one can even figure out how to make amends, ever satisfy a presumably infinite God?

More disturbingly, what if God doesn't seem to be acting fairly and the punishment of humanity does not fit the crime? The story of Job is one such story that raises this very question. As noted before, Job was a righteous man who obeyed God, yet was punished time and again as a test of his piety through a wager that God made with Satan. Satan or "the adversary" is allowed to torment Job in order to reveal whether Job will still remain faithful to God. Job's livestock are destroyed along with his house and children. Job, remains faithful to God amidst pleadings from his friends and wife to curse God for this treatment. So what seems to be punishment to everyone in this story except Job is instead a test that Job must pass, not payback for a sin against God. Yes, Job does pass the test and is rewarded in the end with a new family and twice as much livestock than he started with. Does this payment in the end constitute redemption if there really was no grand sin committed by Job and the punishment wasn't really punishment? And more importantly, does the morally questionable allowance of unjustified torment of Job complicate the way one is to understand redemption as it concerns the divine?

German philosopher, Franz Rosenzweig (1886–1929), may help us make sense of justice as it relates to punishment and redemption as he rethinks the relationship between God, the world, and humans, using the Star of David. The star with its six corners is two overlapping triangles. The first triangle connects God, the universe, and human beings, and the other connects creation, revelation, and redemption. The points of this second triangle intersect between the points of the first, and define the nature of the relationship between God, the universe, and humanity. The relationship between God and the universe is one of creation, the relationship between God and human beings is that of revelation, and the third side of the first triangle that connects the universe and humanity is linked by redemption.

Interestingly, God is involved in the redemptive process indirectly. The love that humans display toward God is expressed in the manner by which they relate to the universe, which contains fellow human beings. We sin against the universe hence we should look to that which we sinned against for redemption. Theologically, Rosenzweig means that the *world* is the vehicle that puts humanity into relationship with God. It is through material relationships in the universe that one's relationship to God is clarified, as all three are connected in the same triangle. The ramification of Rosenzweig's idea of redemption is that it necessarily involves other people but is not accomplished through contemplation of God or prayer to God alone. Through a unique means of revelation, God initiates and bears the burden of the relation with humans. Then it is through humanity's relation with the universe that it can attain redemption and it is that which puts it in proper standing before God (Rosenzweig 2005).

When God is believed to be only indirectly involved with punishment and redemption, the sin/punishment/redemption path can take some unexpected turns. In recent decades we see this route of redemption playing out in the Catholic Church through its dealing with pedophiliac priests. Some of the priests who were accused of molesting children were reported to Bishops, Cardinals, and finally to the Vatican under the assumption that church hierarchy is the proper authority to which these cases should be reported. What has become scandalous is not only the systematic abuse of innocent children but also the circumvention of the civil authorities as appropriate conduits for protection and justice. For a long time the Church claimed legal immunity from civil prosecution under the guise of divine authority. However, its divine authority would presumably refuse to sanction the shuttling of priests who molested young boys to other churches instead of punishing them appropriately. Hence, God may be used instrumentally and indirectly here by the Church to protect itself rather than children.

Further complicating the path from sin to redemption in contemporary culture is the fact that there are simply more types of authorities that can be offended and hence more authorities that can grant redemption in our lives now than in times past. One wonders whether the likes of the 1980s televangelists Jimmy Swaggart and Jim Bakker (both caught cheating on their wives) were merely paying lip service when they asked for forgiveness in front of their congregants *and* a television audience. Who, exactly, did they sin against that demands such a public forum for their contrition? We can presume that they, as evangelical Christians, would consider their sin to be against God primarily, their family secondarily. Certainly their congregation is owed an apology too, but with these scandals involving high-profile ministers, there may be mixed motives driving the public display of emotion. Is their acceptance of responsibility for their transgressions genuine? Are they *really* sorry for what they did? Or are they hoping for their congregants' forgiveness as a sign of their redemption?

The case of megachurch pastor Ted Haggard comes to mind as well. Disgracefully dismissed from the church he founded because of the purchase of crystal meth and a sexual relation with a male prostitute, Haggard has started a new church after claiming to now be redeemed. Yet his old church refused to take him back, signaling that some wounds are too deep for full redemption. Who has the right to grant redemption in these cases? How would we know that God, a congregation, loved ones, or the general public has indeed forgiven them? If Swaggart, Bakker, and Haggard's wives didn't forgive them, then should his congregation? At what point is redemption complete for these pastors when there is no clear biblical script that addresses the myriad authorities that are to be appeased? And is it ever justified for anyone to make such claims of redemption without rock-solid verification?

If all of the categories associated with the process of redemption have become less clear over time, it stands to reason that sin, punishment, and redemption are more open to personal interpretation than in times past. Religious doctrine and biblical injunctions may still provide guidelines and even a roadmap according to which redemption is achieved today. However, what has muddied the waters is the multitude of authorities that can be sinned against, can mete out punishment, and then grant redemption. Even in religious circles, where God is certainly one of those authorities, it may be a reputation and a public image that one is seeking to redeem and not only one's soul.

Hence, God now stands alongside those more secular authorities that can grant such redemption, thus making the entire process of attaining redemption more in need of a roadmap than ever.

Redemption in Religion and Sports

If Freud is right in describing the modern human condition in socio-psychological terms, then there exists a deep cultural contention that we are flawed beings whose rational exterior hides our self-deception from ourselves. Certain aspects of human nature and behavior are uncontrollable both in principle and in practice, and one cannot reach the depths of the human psyche to eradicate all conceivable emotional and conceptual sins, according to the Freudian perspective. Here, the biblical language of sin, punishment, and redemption only deals with *some* aspects of the human being because it is based on the assumption that humans are sinful as revealed through acts performed knowledgeably and freely. But if religion deals with one's actions and thoughts as manifestations of a free subject, then it may not deal as well with hidden fantasies and desires that operate from a place that we have no control over.

Here is where celebrity athletes get caught in a vicious cycle. Even when their words and actions of contrition are accepted by the public at large, they still remain suspect and never fully vindicated or forgiven because no one knows for sure *why* they did what they did and therefore whether they will do it again. Tiger Woods offered what seemed a sincere apology for his infidelity, but when he rhetorically said during his press conference, "I know people want to find out how I could be so selfish and so foolish," he never gave them what they wanted. How are we or anyone else for that matter able to offer forgiveness when the perpetrator doesn't know why the transgression was committed?

And when wrongdoing is institutional *and* individual, as in the case of the Catholic Church, both sin and redemption get even murkier. As is true in many of our examples involving sports and religion, we have a parallel to the sex abuse scandal of the Church in the sports world. The conviction of former Penn State University football assistant coach Jerry Sandusky in 2012 for child molestation ended a year-long scandal for the university. Like the Catholic Church, high level administrators at Penn State as well as the head coach, Joe Paterno, largely ignored accusations against Sandusky even when some of them involved crimes occurring on the campus itself. With both the Catholic Church and Penn State, we have two powerful institutions that have built themselves up on a certain image of honesty and trust with the community. In major sports programs at universities, no less in the Vatican, a crime as serious as child molestation can sadly be minimized in order to protect this image. Despite the fact that one of these institutions has a more explicit connection to matters theological, Penn State is the functional equivalent of the Church. A mural on the campus had Coach Paterno, surrounded by alumni and staff, with a halo above his head, if one doubts this claim.

The Catholic Church and Penn State's crimes are egregious and hence, punishment and the possibility of redemption are put on stage. Yet, we can safely say that Sandusky's crime was worse than the Penn State officials' looking the other way. Sandusky's motives, while twisted, are clear enough, but what of the motives of Paterno and other administrators? While they certainly should have taken the charges with utmost seriousness, they also had the reputation of the university in mind. Their actions cannot be justified morally, but they do call into question the level to which we can be held accountable for actions that follow mixed motives. Can we ever plumb our own depths? And when we do, can anyone see that deep? The reliance on a relationship between humans and God, as Rosenzweig reminds us, depends on our relation with the universe so that an existential dimension remains a precondition for spiritual transcendence. These relations are guided by external laws as well as internal laws that we have imposed on ourselves while being mindful of social and moral principles (biblical and others). So, it makes sense for us to be bound by these laws and in some ways never fully escape their judgment—we cannot circumvent them by merely gaining God's blessing.

If the relationship with God is mediated through relationships with others and ourselves but the ability to understand our own motives (much less those of others) or know which authority to appeal to leaves the means of achieving redemption ambiguous at best in either sports or religion today. Christianity may seem to offer an "easy" way out or a "ready-made" path to salvation, but in fact it requires a deeper reflection into the nature and ramifications of sin. A simple apology offered by the athlete who has messed up may or may not be a step on the road to redemption.

One way to integrate religion and sports together in American culture today is through this ambiguity that both share. The professional athlete and the successful pastor are judged on multiple levels all the time, as are the Church and college sports programs, making them both accountable to multiple authorities. Moreover, it is the overall need for redemption in the face of mistakes made and left unaccounted for that continues to permeate religious and sports discourses. If the source of some of those mistakes is more unclear than it used to be and the search for proper channels to make amends for those mistakes may take the searcher down multiple paths, then, ironically, it may be easier to find points of commonality between the redemption sought in religion and that sought after in sports.

The pursuit of redemption in sports, if only to redeem a stellar career with a late-stage championship, may not appeal to a God for redemption, but the need for it is no less intense than that in many types of religious pursuit of it. Alternatively, the straightforward steps to redemption articulated in some parts of the Bible may not work as well in today's fast-paced world with multiple authorities that often work at cross-purposes. Perhaps it is in sports that we can look for examples of a more unambiguous redemption. Pete Rose finally gets into the Hall of Fame, Tiger Woods wins the Masters again, and the player with impressive stats over a long career finally wins a championship. These are tangible, though perhaps incomplete, markers of redemption in sports that can be contrasted to intangible, perhaps uncertain, markers of redemption in religion. That said, it is the religious notion of redemption—that mistakes need more than simple punishment to make a situation right again—that continues to bring the notion front and center in sports. Again, sports and religion come together on the cultural level around the concept of redemption with both needing each other to help us make sense of a complex concept such as redemption without one discourse taking over or eliminating the need for the other.

CONCLUSION

Our treatment of several important themes in this book demonstrates that sports and religion in American culture are not really in conflict, despite the still-held belief that one has little to do with the other or that one has gained cultural supremacy over the other. Our assessment would be the exact opposite one given of the relationship between religion and sports a mere 20 years ago. One discourse is sacred, one is secular and the two really have nothing to say to each other while the secular quietly wins this battle, so the old way of thinking goes. The fact that religion has not only refused to disappear but has also strengthened in many locations shows that new approaches to the relationship between traditionally secular institutions, such as sports, and religion were and are still needed in this postsecular environment of ours.

If one approach to the relationship sees religion and sports moving around on the same plane of the same cultural web, then each is able to utilize the same logic and expressions to achieve its own separate objectives in the cultural arena. Therefore, we should find some of the same linguistic expressions, goals, and themes in both that inform the use in each other's discourses. Tim Tebow can seamlessly move between talking about the religious type of belief and the belief in his teammates without having to parse out which discourse he is leaning on at any given time. A trek to Wrigley Field can rightly be called a pilgrimage without concern for trespassing on an exclusively religious meaning of the term. And the time and effort spent in the gym can reveal that the religion behind a strong work ethic can find different expression when religion can no longer motivate hard work. All of these examples suggest that religion and sports work with each other at times in ways that reflect a postsecular relationship between the two.

In fact, postsecularism opens up all kinds of new horizons for the study of religion and as such, several insights follow from our own inquiry into religion and sports and its admitted limitations. Expanding on our own examination, first we suggest that the interplay between religion and sports can be duplicated in a relationship between other cultural manifestations. One can compare religion and music or religion and movies, just to name a few, and find similarities and differences ranging from the financial pressures that permeate both industries to the characters and principles that animate each expression. When comparing any secular cultural expression to a religious one, it should become evident that religious ideas and ethics remain paramount in Western culture as they inform so many facets of our lives, even when we are unaware of this influence.

Because our intention was to address religion and sports in America generally, we refrained from engaging in what is commonly known as "identity politics." That means that questions of race, gender, sexuality, and class, while essential to most academic treatments of social interactions, were not discussed in detail. Though examples were given in some chapters, we hold, second, that these identifying distinctions may furnish future scholars with further applications of the postsecular framework to narrower fields of study as it relates to sports and religion.

Third, just as we focused on the Bible and Western culture, one could just as easily bring into play other Western religious traditions or religions and philosophies of the East or South and undertake similar analyses as they concern any sports scene. What emerges from our study is the ongoing conversation that contemporary culture has with its past. And this past inevitably includes religious beliefs and practices whose remnants can be uncovered if one is looking in the right place. It may be as simple as the socialized reverence of the East that has filtered into the United States or the custodial approach towards nature embodied in Native American religions that bears heavily on the norms and values of American sports. The limiting of ourselves to the religions of the Bible as positioned in American culture merely lights *one* path that can lead to other paths that are informed by other sacred texts honored around the globe.

Fourth, though our focus on contemporary culture assumes a certain capitalist mode of social interaction driven by profit-optimization and marketplace forces of supply and demand, this doesn't mean that a different economic arrangement could not be put into relationship with American religion quite easily. We encourage the reader to examine other political–economic frameworks, from outright socialism to hybrid capitalism (state-capitalism in China, for example), and analyze the extent to which religion and sports or religion and whatever cultural expression find themselves coexisting. However unique the American experience may be, it's not unique enough that a parallel experience is lacking in other political/economic arrangements.

In addition to acting as a springboard for future, more varied studies, our project, to repeat once more, yields several important conclusions. One, since we are all living in a postsecular and postmodern world, where clear lines of separation between discourses and practices are not as strict as they were before, we are able to move seamlessly from the sacred to the profane and back again. Two, because of this seamless movement, we no longer have to choose between religion and sports, as if one negates the other, but can engage both as they inform and utilize many of the same concepts and institutions. Three, once you engage both as equals, you are more likely than otherwise to transport ideas and principles from one to the other to the mutual benefit of both. Four, as you transport ideas from one area of your life to the other, you tend to use similar vocabulary and therefore blur the difference that often still delineates the two discourses thus feeding the postsecular mindset. And five, once the hierarchy between the two is undermined as is the priority of the one over the other (historically, ontologically, epistemologically), new interpretative horizons open up that allow for novel applications.

Yet these new horizons are not afloat in a relativist chaos where any arrangement between sports and religion will suffice. Though open-ended, which leaves greater room for maneuvering, the relationship between religion and sports in a postsecular context is, perhaps ironically, accompanied by an additional sense of responsibility. Whatever you do and however you do it, whether playing ball with your friends or joining a local group of worshippers, you must become more, not less mindful of the different contexts that now pervade American society and what they expect of you. One's own interpretation and behavior should express the recognition of the interplay of religion and sports as two important parts of the lives of many. Religion does not lose its seriousness when associated with sports in this way, nor does sports lose its edge when it is admitted that historically religious themes are found to be animating some of the actions on the field. You can have them both, enjoy what they offer you, and in return, ensure that you respectfully pay homage to their respective contributions.

In the twenty-first century, as postsecularists suggest, religion remains a crucial social enterprise that encourages people to transcend their daily existence as a way to reflect on their personal commitments and conviction, their behavior towards others, and their place in the universe. As such, religion offers an invitation for engagement and a testing ground for communities claiming to nurture love and understanding among people with grace and charity as embedded ways of relating to one another. With this in mind, religion can retain its relevance as a carrier of values and ideals. When religious institutions forget their mission and significance in human affairs, they can ideally be reminded of their boundaries by other institutions, such as sports, that are able to perform similar functions in, at times, more culturally relevant ways. In this way, sports can ground religion when it loses its way. Reciprocally, religion can ground sports when it is unable to provide the codes of living that it has typically been able to transmit. They need each other, inform each other, and challenge each other—hopefully to the mutual benefit of all.

BIBLIOGRAPHY

Albanese, Catherine (1992), *America, Religions and Religion*, Belmont, CA: Wadsworth.

Asad, Talal (2003), *Formations of the Secular: Christianity, Islam, Modernity*, Stanford, CA: Stanford University Press.

Baker, William J. (2007), *Playing with God: Religion and Modern Sport*, Cambridge, MA: Harvard University Press.

Bellah, Robert N. (2011), *Religion in Human Evolution: From the Paleolithic to the Axial Age*, Cambridge, MA: Harvard University Press.

Berger, Peter (1967), *The Sacred Canopy: Elements of a Sociological Theory of Religion*, New York: Anchor Books.

Bloom, Harold (1992), *The American Religion: The Emergence of the Post-Christian Nation*, New York: Simon & Schuster.

Bonhoeffer, Dietrich (1995), *The Cost of Discipleship*, New York: Touchstone Press.

Brooks, David (2012), "The Jeremy Lin Problem," *The New York Times*, February 16, 2012.

Bunyan, John (2009), *The Pilgrim's Progress*, New York: Penguin.

Calvin, John (1960), *Institutes of the Christian Religion, vol. 2*, Philadelphia, PA: Westminster John Knox Press.

Casanova, José (2006), "Rethinking Secularization: Global Comparative Perspective," *The Hedgehog Review*, vol. 8, no. 1/2, 7–22.

Chidester, David (1996), "The Church of Baseball, the Fetish of Coca-Cola, & the Potlatch of Rock 'n' Roll: Theoretical Models of the Study of

Religion in Popular American Culture," *Journal of the American Academy of Religion*, vol. LXIV/4, 743–765.

Covey, Stephen R. (2004), *The 8th Habit: From Effectiveness to Greatness*, New York: Free Press.

Craft, Kevin (2011), "The Refreshing Seriousness of Tim Tebow," *The Atlantic*, November 28, 2011.

Curry, Jack (2004), "Rose, in New Book, Admits Betting on His Team," *The New York Times*, January 6, 2004.

de Vries, Hent and Lawrence E. Sullivan (2006), *Political Theologies: Public Religions in a Post-secular World*, eds. Hent de Vries and Lawrence E. Sullivan, New York: Fordham University Press.

Douthat, Ross (2012), "Tebow in Babylon," *The New York Times*, March 24, 2012.

Edwards, Harry (1973), *Sociology of Sport*, Homewood, IL: Dorsey Press.

Evans, Christopher H. and William R. Herzog II (2002), *The Faith of 50 Million: Baseball, Religion and American Culture*, Louisville, KY: Westminster John Knox Press.

Forbes, Bruce David and Jeffrey H. Mahan (2000), *Religion and Popular Culture in America*, Berkeley, CA: University of California Press.

Forney, Craig A. (2010), *The Holy Trinity of American Sports: Civil Religion in Football, Baseball, and Basketball*, Macon, GA: Mercer University Press.

Foucault, Michel (1970), *The Order of Things: An Archeology of the Human Sciences*, New York: Vintage Books.

—— (1979), *Discipline and Punish: The Birth of the Prison*, translated by Alan Sheridan, New York: Vintage Books.

Freud, Sigmund (1961), *Civilization and Its Discontents*, translated and edited by James Strachey, New York: W. W. Norton & Company.

Geertz, Clifford (1977), *The Interpretation of Cultures*, New York: Basic Books.

Guttmann, Allen (1978), *From Ritual to Record: The Nature of Modern Sports*, New York: Columbia University Press.

Higgs, Robert J. (1995), *God in the Stadium: Sports and Religion in America*, Lexington, KY: University of Kentucky Press.

Higgs, Robert J. and Michael C. Braswell (2004), *An Unholy Alliance: The Sacred and Modern Sports*, Macon, GA: Mercer University Press.

Hoffman, Shirl (2010), *Good Game: Christianity and the Culture of Sports*, Waco, TX: Baylor University Press.

Hubeart, T. L. Jr. (1996), "Glenn Gould and the Electronic Future," www.pennuto.com/music/gould.htm.

James, William (1956), *The Will to Believe and Other Essays in Popular Philosophy*, New York: Dover Publications.

Jhally, Sut (1989), "Media Sports, Culture and Power: Critical Issues in the Communication of Sport," in *Media, Sports, and Society: Research on the*

Communication of Sport, ed. Lawrence A. Wenner, Newbury Park, CA: Sage, 70–93.

Kindred, Dave (2011), "Revisiting Rose: Sportswriters Examine Exile of Reds Great, 22 Years Later," Indiana University, National Sports Journalism Center, August 8, 2011.

Klosterman, Chuck (2011), "The People Who Hate Tim Tebow," www.grantland.com/story/_/id/7319858/the-people-hate-tim-tebow, December 6, 2011.

Lyotard, Jean-François (1984), *The Postmodern Condition: A Report on Knowledge*, translated by Geoff Bennington and Brian Massumi, Minneapolis, MN: University of Minnesota Press.

Marx, Karl (1976), *Capital: A Critique of Political Economy, vol. 1*, translated by Ben Fowkes, New York: Vintage Books.

Morgan, William J. (1994), *Leftist Theories of Sport: A Critique and Reconstruction*, Urbana, Il: University of Illinois Press.

Novak, Michael (1994), *The Joy of Sports: End Zones, Bases, Baskets, Balls, and the Consecration of the American Spirit*, Lanham, MD: Rowman & Littlefield.

Ostwalt, Conrad (2003), *Secular Steeples: Popular Culture and the Religious Imagination*, New York: Continuum.

Overman, Steven (2011), *The Protestant Ethic and the Spirit of Sport*, Macon, GA: Mercer University Press.

Prebish, Charles S. (1993), *Religion and Sport: The Meeting of Sacred and Profane*, Westport, CT: Greenwood Press.

Price, Joseph L., ed. (2001), *From Season to Season: Sports as American Religion*, Macon, GA: Mercer University Press.

—— (2006), *Rounding the Bases: Baseball and Religion in America*, Macon, GA: Mercer University Press.

Roenigk, Alyssa (2010), http://sports.espn.go.com/espn/news/story?id=5660039.

Rosenzweig, Franz (2005), *The Star of Redemption*, translated by Barbara E. Galli, Madison, WI: University of Wisconsin Press.

Rudnyckyj, Daromir (2010), *Spiritual Economies: Islam, Globalization, and the Afterlife of Development*, Ithaca, NY: Cornell University Press.

Scholes, Jeffrey (2005), "The Bartman Ball and Sacrifice: Ambiguity in an American Ritual," *Journal of Religion and Society*, vol. 7, 1–13.

Sexton, John with Thomas Oliphant and Peter J. Schwartz (2013), *Baseball as a Road to God: Seeing Beyond the Game*, New York: Gotham Books.

Smith, Greg (2010), *Sports Theology: Playing Inside Out*, Indianapolis, IN: Dog Ear Publishing.

Stark, Rodney and William Sims Bainbridge (1985), *The Future of Religion: Secularization, Revival and Cult Formation*, Berkeley, CA: University of California Press.

Taylor, Charles (2007), *A Secular Age*, Cambridge and London: Harvard University Press.

Turner, Bryan S. (2012), "Post-Secular Society: Consumerism and the Democratization of Religion," in *The Post-Secular in Question: Religion in Contemporary Society*, eds., Philip Gorski, David Kyuman Kim, John Torpey, and Jonathan Van Anntwerpen, New York: New York University Press, 135–158.

Twitchell, James and Ken Ross (2008), *Where Men Hide*, New York: Columbia University Press.

Van Biema, David and Jeff Chu (2006), "Does God Want You to Be Rich?", *Time Magazine*, www.time.com/time/magazine/article/0,9171,1533448-1,00.html, September 10, 2006.

Warren, Rick (2003), *The Purpose-Driven Life: What on Earth Am I Here For?*, Grand Rapids, MI: Zondervan.

Weber, Max (1905/1958), *The Protestant Ethic and the Spirit of Capitalism*, translated by Talcott Parsons, New York: Charles Scribner's Sons.

Weideman, Reeves (2011), "Defending Tebow," *The New Yorker*, November 18, 2011.

Williams, Serena (2006), "Wimbledon Has Sent Me a Message: I'm Only a Second Class Champion," *New York Times*, June 26, 2006.

Wuthnow, Robert (1998), *After Heaven: Spirituality in America Since the 1950s*, Berkeley, CA: University of California Press.

—— (2007), "Secularisation and the Future of Christianity: Lessons from the American Experience," in *Christianity in the Post Secular West*, eds., John Stenhouse and Brett Knowles, Hindmarsh, South Australia: Australasian Theological Forum Press, 27–51.

INDEX